STRANGE
and
OBSCURE STORIES
of
NEW YORK CITY

STRANGE
and
OBSCURE STORIES
of
NEW YORK CITY

Little-Known Tales about
Gotham's People and Places

By Tim Rowland

Skyhorse Publishing

Skyhorse Publishing books may be purchased in bulk at special discounts for sales promotion, corporate gifts, fund-raising, or educational purposes. Special editions can also be created to specifications. For details, contact the Special Sales Department, Skyhorse Publishing, 307 West 36th Street, 11th Floor, New York, NY 10018, or info@skyhorsepublishing.com.

Skyhorse® and Skyhorse Publishing® are registered trademarks of Skyhorse Publishing, Inc.®, a Delaware corporation.

Visit our website at www.skyhorsepublishing.com.

10 9 8 7 6 5 4 3 2 1

Library of Congress Cataloging-in-Publication Data is available on file.

Cover design by Jane Sheppard
Cover photos: iStockphoto

Print ISBN: 978-1-5107-0012-3
Ebook ISBN: 978-1-5107-0013-0

Printed in the United States of America

To Beth, for believing in me more than I believe in myself.

Table of Contents

Preface   ix

CHAPTER 1
Selling the Public on a Jump from the Brooklyn Bridge   1

CHAPTER 2
A Humble Printer Establishes Freedom of the Press   13

CHAPTER 3
Botched Abortion, Botched Justice   27

CHAPTER 4
The US Mail Underfoot   39

CHAPTER 5
The Grand Slave Conspiracy that Wasn't   55

CHAPTER 6
Mark Twain Takes New York by Storm and Spirit   69

CHAPTER 7
The Rise and Fall of Little Germany   81

CHAPTER 8
New York's Cross-Dressing Governor   93

CHAPTER 9
A Deadly Battle of Shakespearean Actors   103

CHAPTER 10
Woodlawn Cemetery's Celebrated Clientele   113

CHAPTER 11
A Building and a Food Fight for the Ages   129

CHAPTER 12
New York's New Insane Classes, and the Woman
Who Fought for Them   143

CHAPTER 13
New York Declares War on Pigs   157

CHAPTER 14
A Floating City of Liquor   165

CHAPTER 15
A Lake Gets Its Revenge on Manhattan   181

Sources   193

Preface

In New York City, it goes without saying, strange stories are a dime a dozen. The chore is not to ferret them out, the chore is to narrow the selection down. Obscure stories are harder to find, since the city is blessed with an uncountable amount of excellent books, blogs, and websites that have dutifully catalogued and chronicled just about everything that's happened in New York since the Earth cooled.

So if the historical essays presented here are more strange than they are obscure, this is why. It is hoped, however, that they will add layers and context that give added meaning and amusement to readers, even if they have heard in passing that, say, New York had a cross-dressing governor or that the US mail once sailed along in tubes buried beneath city sidewalks.

What is also striking is the degree to which New York reflects the nation at large. Yankees though they might have been, the city had slave riots that rivaled anything in the South, and at the time of the Civil War, Mayor Fernando Wood even agitated for secession from the Union.

New Yorkers were at the fore in undercutting prohibition. They witnessed a steamboat demonstration that predated Robert Fulton's by twenty years. The rhetoric of its leaders in commerce soared to the stars and set the tone for the nation, yet it produced criminals so shameless and rank that it was hard to think of them as human.

A *maître d'* in New York could accumulate more fame and adoration than a deacon in any other town. In everything from architecture, to design, to sports, to politics, New York set the standard—it might not always have been a pretty standard, but it was a standard that could never be ignored. So if its stories (even the obscure ones) are strange, wonderful, and, like the city itself, they cannot be ignored.

CHAPTER 1

Selling the Public on a Jump from the Brooklyn Bridge

In all probability, on a midsummer day in 1886, a twenty-five-year-old man named Steve Brodie joined thousands of other New Yorkers by not jumping off the Brooklyn Bridge. No matter. The young huckster from the Bowery parlayed this nonevent into a storied career that lives on in the annals of history, pop culture, and showmanship. There is, however, just that chance that he did jump; like Brodie himself, that facts that surround that July day are hopelessly complex.

The Brooklyn Bridge had been completed in 1883, and the engineering marvel had captured the imagination of New Yorkers almost from the day that it was proposed in a set of improbable architectural sketches. Dubbed one of the Seven Wonders of the Industrial World, one hundred and fifty thousand pedestrians and eighteen hundred vehicles crossed the bridge into history on its opening day. A week later, a rumor spread that the massive stone structure was in imminent danger of collapse. The news caused a stampede that killed a dozen people. Sensing an opportunity, the legendary P. T. Barnum later paraded twenty-one elephants across the bridge to prove its stability.

But with a height of 135 feet, equal to a fourteen-story building, from the decking to the water, the bridge quickly attracted the attention of daredevils, who contemplated the odds of leaping from the bridge and surviving.

The first was Robert Emmet Odlum, a swimming instructor from a family torn by the Civil War, who taught aquatic skills to the children of such luminaries as Rutherford B. Hayes, James Garfield, and William T. Sherman. Always seeking new challenges, Odlum transitioned from endurance swimming into high-diving. He escaped unharmed, more or less, from dives off a ninety-foot bridge near Washington, DC, and a ladder affixed to a steamship 110 feet high. Meanwhile, as he was plummeting to the depths below, so was his business. His swimming school, while critically acclaimed, failed, and his proffered side bets on how far he could swim found no takers. He was one of those whose success in life never seemed to translate into financial reward; he won applause for his swimming feats, and as a hotel lifeguard he was credited with the ocean rescue of Sky Colfax, son of Lincoln's Vice President Schuyler Colfax—but these heroics weren't paying the bills. Odlum reckoned a jump from the celebrated Brooklyn Bridge might be the ticket to success, and he began to make plans for just such an event.

Unfortunately, the police got wind of the stunt, and the chief police inspector put out the word to be on the lookout for suspicious activity. Odlum's mother would later say that her boy's motives were pure; he wanted to prove that the rushing air of a fall was not, in itself, fatal. This, she said, would convince the men and women trapped in the upper floors of a burning building to be at ease jumping into a fire net. And, of course, if he happened to parlay the daredevil act into a little coin, well, what woman in those days couldn't use a little cash?

On the nineteenth of May 1885, Robert Odlum got out of bed and went to church to confess his sins. Everything else was in place. He'd hired a strong swimmer stationed on a tugboat to come to his aid after the jump, as well as a body double whose job was to bait the police into chasing down the wrong guy. At a little after five in the afternoon, the radar on the Brooklyn Bridge's toll collector wiggled to life. A carriage carrying a man in a skin-tight blue shirt passed through the gate, with a second man who appeared to be attempting to screen his companion. And the cab was going way too fast; something was up. At the toll keeper's signal, a dozen watchmen scampered after Odlum. The police weren't the only ones on high alert for the jump. With stunning quickness, a crowd of thousands materialized out of nowhere. Part of the problem, the newspapers said later, was that the police themselves had spread word of the impending "crazy scheme," hoping that many would be on hand to view their heroics as they stopped this insane individual from certain death. As PR goes, it was a fair effort, except that the gathering crowd made it impossible for police to do their job. The *Times* wrote that the "Bluecoats could be seen from the roadway making an ado above, in utterly useless attempts to keep the crowd in motion." The cops closed in on the suspected jumper from all sides. "They were determined that the cab should not get close enough to the rail on the river side for the best leaper in the world to jump."

There was no doubt in the minds of the police that the mysterious man in the cab was indeed Odlum. If any further proof was needed, a tug of cheering fans churned up the river, spectators affixing spyglasses on the bridge in search of their hero's profile against the sky. The whole affair seemed to play out in slow motion, the cab and the police inching along through a sea of derby-hatted humanity. The blue-shirted man grew increasingly nervous, more from the chase, perhaps, than the thought of the jump. He fumbled cartoonishly with the collar of his shirt, as officers got within an arm's length of the cab. According to the *Times*, "The commotion in the vicinity of the cab had become tumultuous; other vehicles pressed close behind; the crowd was clamorous and excited overhead; the middle of the bridge had been reached, and the people in the tugboat were intently watching the bridge." But as dogged as the cab driver had been, the police had been even more determined. Relentlessly, they began to form a line of blue between the cab and the rail of the Brooklyn Bridge. It was as they had hoped. The crowd would be treated to the sight of New York's finest in action, and there were plenty of self-satisfied smiles all around as the police finally took the cab into custody.

So intent was everyone's attention on the cab that few noticed when a trim man in a red shirt stepped from a nondescript wagon and hopped lightly upon the bridge's railing, raising his right hand to the sky. The police, the spectators in the tug, *everyone*, had been watching the wrong man. So relieved had the toll keeper been at spotting that man who he thought was Odlum that he had subsequently let down his guard. "The ordinary black covered wagon in which Odlum got access to the bridge had nothing about it to suggest suspicion," said the *Times*. "It moved along with the slow line, its three occupants sitting quietly within, looking as though that was where they belonged." Had the toll keeper been a whisper sharper, he might have noticed the glint of a showman's outfit peeking out from under the standard workman's garb. But in fact, it hardly mattered—Odlum was one determined man.

A jump from the height represented by the Brooklyn Bridge is survivable, but only if everything goes right. The key is to hit the water ramrod straight, and Odlum didn't, quite. Some blamed the wind. Others said that the haste in which he exited the wagon and leapt to the rail destroyed his balance. Whatever, Odlum was several degrees off plumb and smacked the water with a sound that could be heard over the noise of the crowd. When the great swimmer surfaced, he was face down and wasn't moving. Odlum was pulled, unconscious, into the tug, and laid out in the galley. Brandy, the catch-all medicine of the day, was poured down his throat. The liquor revived him somewhat, and faintly he asked, "What kind of jump did I make?" Everyone assured him that he'd nailed it. He struggled to sit up, and for a beat, it seemed as if he might survive. Then blood began to dribble from the corner of his mouth. "Am I spitting blood?" he asked. No, he was assured, it was just the brandy coming back up. It wasn't, of course. His liver, spleen, and most of his other internal organs had ruptured on impact. An hour after his jump, he was dead.

If nothing else, Odlum set the table for whoever might jump next, and live. That honor most likely went to a fellow by the name of Larry Donovan, a chap who received zero credit for his exploit. Seeking a suitable sobriquet for a specimen such as himself, Donovan, not wishing to aim low, had settled on "the Champion Aerial Jumper of the World." On April 18, 1887, the champion of the world determined to jump from the bridge, and alerted the press to his impending feat. The press, being the press, immediately raced to his mother's home so that they would be present to dutifully record the look on her face when she received word of her son's death. But the woman wasn't home. She was down at the police station, tipping off the cops regarding her son's shenanigans.

In the history of superheroes, it is possible, perhaps, to conceive of a more ignominious fate than that of young Donovan. If Superman's mommy, for example, had pointed out a hole in his shorts prior to his impending rescue of Lois Lane. But for the Champion Aerial Jumper of the world, this embarrassment only hardened his resolve. On August 28, 1886, Donovan, a typesetter by trade, leapt from the Brooklyn Bridge and survived. History little remembers him, perhaps because in less than two years he was dead himself, victim of a failed attempt to jump from the Hungerford Bridge over the River Thames in London. But more likely it's because when he jumped, the feat was thought to be old news—a month prior, Steve Brodie had won the honor for himself, or so everyone thought.

Unlike Odlum before him, Brodie, a twenty-three-year-old former paperboy from the Bowery, did not seem to duck attention as he stood on the New York side of the bridge on July 23, 1886. He may have, however, been every bit as deceitful. The story was that he'd made a $200 bet—about $5,000 today—that he could survive a leap into the river (the price for such a stunt had risen substantially following the publicity surrounding Odlum's death). A young woman spoke loudly—maybe a little too loudly—as she bid farewell to the daredevil: "Good-bye Steve; take care of yourself and may you be successful and scoop in dose two huntrid dollars so's we kin have a good time," quoted the *Times*.

Brodie also needed the cash to cover some unfortunate bets he had made of late at the horse track, it was whispered. Brodie loved to gamble, and had earned some decent money as a professional speedwalker (a popular endurance sport in the nineteenth century known as pedestrianism; events could last for days, and were subject to heavy wagering among the betting public). When that pursuit had become dull, Brodie had turned to high-diving, and he carried with him clippings documenting his jumps. Bridge jumping came naturally, as Brodie had been a lifeguard in his early years, reportedly saving a number of lives, including that of a young woman who gave him her locket as a keepsake.

As Brodie parted from his sweetie *du jour* on the day of the jump (a woman who was not his wife, it would turn out), he hopped aboard a lumber wagon, and the police officer stationed at the toll house either failed to notice Brodie or was indifferent. Or perhaps he failed to recognize Brodie for the simple reason that the young man was not Brodie at all. Even today, no one is sure. At the time, it seemed real enough. The *Times* reported that, as multiple people reached up to pull him back, Brodie scampered up and over the rail and then grabbed the underside of a girder and hung over the river. "Brodie swung to and fro in the breeze, and he steadied himself as well as he could. When he hung perpendicularly over the river he let go his hold and shot down like an arrow," the paper said. He hit the water in a standing position, for the most part, and disappeared beneath the surface for several seconds. His friends had been waiting in a rowboat below, and when Brodie surfaced, dazed, they fished him out and assessed his condition.

Finding him no worse for wear, he was transported to shore, where he was more than happy to wave to the rapidly growing crowd and speak with the waiting press. Not so impressed with his performance was the bridge officer, who immediately placed New York's newest hero under arrest. A soaking wet Brodie was taken to the nearest precinct station. Appearing pale and blue-lipped, a sympathetic officer gave the young man a pull on his whiskey bottle. This seemed to revive the shivering diver, who sent a newspaper reporter to fetch him a fresh pint. The police—not wanting the perp to show up for court drunk—were disinclined to allow him any more, but when Brodie clutched his side, wailed in pain, and went into convulsions, they relented. A doctor was called, who checked Brodie out and declared him fit as a fiddle, a diagnosis that Brodie celebrated with more whiskey. Seeing that Brodie was consuming so much liquor under the watchful eyes of the men in blue, it hardly seemed fair when they took him to the city prison on a charge of intoxication, along with endangering his own life.

Prison wardens in those days felt no particular need to prohibit newspaper reporters from wandering the cellblocks, and a correspondent from the *Times* struck up a conversation with the new celebrity, deciphering, as best he was able, Brodie's heavy

Bowery accent, his slurred speech, and his truly impressive command of contemporary profanity. Other reporters quickly tracked down Brodie's wife, who said she had known nothing about it until an hour after the fact. This made the good-bye wishes from the young woman on the bridge prior to the jump a little problematic—not that Brodie was a traditionalist in his relationships with women; he was once arrested for kidnapping and attempting to marry a sixteen-year-old girl. His wife also said that the injury to his side, which had been attributed to the jump, was an old malady that Brodie frequently complained of. Back in the Bowery, Brodie, wrote the *Times*, "is regarded as a sort of half-witted fellow by his friends, a man who will undertake anything if provoked or offered money."

However, if he were indeed half-witted, then what to say of the people he supposedly duped that day? The skeptics believed that Brodie arranged to have a dummy tossed from the bridge, and then swam to general vicinity either from shore or from the rowboat. This was partly based on the comments of a friend, forty years after the fact, and well after Brodie's death, who suggested the jump was all an act. Yet the evidence to support it being a fraud is largely second hand, and more than a century later doesn't seem any more convincing than the first-hand accounts at the time, which did not question the authenticity.

If Brodie was a skilled jumper, he was even better at getting his name out before an enchanted public. He made the rounds of dime museums and traveled the country jumping off of high places, which was a lucrative way to make a living at the time, apparently. With his substantial earnings, he opened a saloon in the Bowery, which became something of a shrine to neighborhood boxers and fighters. This "den of iniquity," as the papers framed it, was scorned by the city's upper crust, as was his taste in younger women, some of them fresh out of reform school. But he was a hero to his people. He fed many a hungry person, distributed umbrellas to shop girls on rainy days, and, when all else failed, paid the funeral expenses for those who died on the street without identification. And if the press wished to write up any stories of his largesse, he never seemed to object.

Brodie grew into the personification of the rough and tumble, vice-riddled Bowery itself. His celebrity was eventually transformed to the stage, and he starred in the play "On the Bowery," which enjoyed a national following. From there it was on to musicals (where he sang about his "Bowery Goyls") and national tours. He was onstage in Cleveland in 1898 when he collapsed, struggled to his feet, and collapsed again. The crowd hissed, thinking him to be drunk, always a viable supposition when it came to Brodie. In fact, he had been battling a bout of pleurisy, and had just telegraphed his family, telling them that he'd be home to recuperate. He never made it. His daughter was awaiting his arrival when she received the telegram reporting his death at age forty.

Brodie's memory lived on long after he did, and throughout the twentieth century the phrase "taking a Brody (sic)" came to mean anything involving a suicidal jump. In pop culture, Brodie's character was invoked in everything from Broadway musicals, to literature, to cinema, to a Bugs Bunny cartoon, where, in trying to sell a tourist the Brooklyn Bridge, "Bowery Bugs" tells the story of how he tormented Brodie into jumping.

Interestingly, sometimes the alleged dummy-double is written into these works, and sometimes it isn't. In the 1933 film *The Bowery*, which covers both bases, Brodie intends to use a dummy, but has to make the jump himself when the figure is stolen by his rival. The 1965 Broadway musical *Kelly* was inspired by Brodie's life and, fittingly, perhaps, wound up being just as controversial.

Anticipating that the production would make quite a splash, so to speak, no expense was spared in anticipation of opening night. For publicity, chorus girls lined up on the Brooklyn Bridge itself, and investors poured money into every phase of production. But with so much at stake, tensions began to run high. In dry runs in Philadelphia and Boston, scenes were rewritten, respected actors Ella Logan, Jack Creley, and Avery Schreiber found their roles had been cut, and arguments over the script flared, almost to the opening curtain. *Kelly* ran for a grand total of one night, imploding in a sea of infighting and financial stresses and making it one of Broadway's greatest flops. The great *Times* critic Howard Taubman, for one, was not sorry to see it go, writing, "Ella Logan was written out of *Kelly* before it reached the Broadhurst Theater Saturday night. Congratulations, Miss Logan."

The show, perhaps fittingly, had pulled a Brody.

CHAPTER 2

A Humble Printer Establishes
Freedom of the Press

Since the dawn of time, the world has not lacked for people who were down on their luck. In the late seventeenth century, one such group would come to be known as the German Palatines of the Middle Rhine. Residents of this scenic river gorge had been repeatedly beaten down by French invaders, and the erstwhile wealthy region was wracked by devastation, famine, and military conscription. The last straw was a winter so extreme that birds were said to have frozen to death as they flew, and even the wine turned to ice in its casks. Much of the life that the Palatines had known was gone, and in the early 1700s, thirteen thousand of them picked up and left, migrating to the safety of England and Ireland.

While sympathetic, the British were somewhat at a loss with how to manage this wave of immigrants; the situation was not unlike the immigration issues that face the world today. But while the British Isles might have been too crowded, across the Atlantic there was more land than anyone knew what to do with, and so, in 1710, three thousand German immigrants boarded ten ships and headed to New York, their hard passage to be paid off by hard work.

Among these refugees were Conrad Weiser, a celebrated emissary between the Indians and colonists; Johann Peter Rockefeller, progenitor of the American Rockefeller family; and a thirteen-year-old boy named Peter Zenger who—little could he have known—was about to form the foundation upon which America's celebrated freedom of the press would be built.

Nor could anyone at the time have likely guessed that the New York City of the early 1700s was on its way to becoming, well, New York City. In 1734, it was a town of ten thousand residents, and nearly two of every 10 were slaves. There might have been just north of fifteen hundred homes, and sporting gentlemen were still able to shoot quail on the east side of Broadway. The city's role at that point was little more than a way station for supplies destined for the interior and American product on its way to British ports.

Little business was transacted within the city itself, and in 1720 it had need of only one newspaper, the *New York Weekly Gazette*, a sheet of foolscap the size of a dinner menu that mainly brought news of more important events in more important locales abroad. The *Gazette* was dutifully loyal to the Crown and the Crown's appointments at a time and place when most people had better things to do than fret over politics. As such, this era might be thought of as the calm before a three-century storm. But attitudes changed with the royal appointment of William Cosby to the governor's palace in 1732. The forty-two-year-old Cosby interrupted what had been a colorless line of British and Dutch bureaucrats of comparatively even temperament and competence.

If the average immigrant to American shores in the colonial period came because of opportunity and religious freedom, the average governor came to American shores because he was broke. Columbia law professor Eben Moglen noted that "The baggage of Governor Cosby, upon his arrival on August 1, 1732, contained two predominant and often-associated guises for an office-holder of his time and place: high socio-political connections at home, and a desperate need for money."

In the Old World, it was all about one's title; in the New World, it was all about cash. In subsequent years, culminating with Alexis de Tocqueville, Europeans visiting American shores remarked with equal parts amazement and disgust that the single-minded pursuit of money was the native population's chief objective. If this were truly the case, it might be because members of all classes saw America as a potential ATM. Cosby, at least, actually laid eyes on the lands he was to govern; some appointees never did even that, preferring to send someone else to run the colony, satisfied to sit at home and cash the paychecks that the position afforded. Almost from the day he set foot in New York, a fair number of his new constituents wished the greedy and litigious Cosby had steered a similar course.

Among Cosby's first acts was to tear up an agreement with the Mohawk Indians that protected their interests, but interfered with the new governor's plan to sell off land patents. The new governor also became embroiled in a legal dispute with his predecessor, Rip Van Dam, over pay; fired judges who failed to rule in his favor; created courts of dubious legality so as to avoid juries; and brought libel suits against his critics.

By stacking the judicial deck, Cosby won in the court of law but suffered grievously in the court of public opinion.

"It is easy to understand what a ferment these proceedings caused," wrote eighteenth-century historian Livingston Rutherford. "Here was a native of the Colony (Van Dam), a man who was rich, influential, and popular, who was well known and respected, forced into expensive litigation by a grasping and unscrupulous governor who denied him common justice, who was, in reality, attempting to help himself to the property of a private citizen, and who hesitated at nothing which he thought would aid him in accomplishing his purpose."

If Cosby expected the slow and steady Van Dam to roll over, he was mistaken. Van Dam rallied his supporters, writing, "We are Tenants at will to Governors, and exposed to be fleeced by them from time to time at their pleasure." Van Dam accused the governor of buying supporters by "Plying them with drink," and, in answer to Cosby's libel suits, said he "did not pretend to know the law" but that he would assume truth to be an air-tight defense. That theory was about to be tested.

New York was increasingly polarized, with the royally appointed Crosby on one side and the popularly elected assembly on the other, including Van Dam, Lewis Morris, Lewis Morris Jr. (the faction would become known as the Morrisites), James Alexander, and William Smith. The ire of the opposition was a microcosm of the grievances that would boil over forty years later at Lexington and Concord, and a letter of Alexander's to a friend in England could have been considered prophetic when he wrote, "(New Yorkers) are generally industrious, the greatest number of them Dutch, and seldom trouble their heads with politics, but such people are generally most violent when they apprehend their liberties are properties to be in danger."

Into this cauldron stepped the young, ne'er-do-well printer, John Peter Zenger. Far more concerned with making a living than with making history, the young man had found conditions in the New World only moderately better than those he had escaped. His father had perished on the journey across the sea, and when his family landed in New York the boy was apprenticed to William Bradford, owner of the *Gazette*. When released from his eight-year term, Zenger wandered south to Maryland, where he dabbled in printing without any particular success. He returned to New York and partnered with Bradford in a publishing concern where they together printed a grand total of one book.

From there he opened his own shop on William, and later Broad Street, several blocks south of City Hall. There, he published a handful of unremarkable books and political pamphlets and was headed for historical oblivion when Cosby's opponents decided they needed to start their own newspaper to get the word out about the governor's atrocities. To print the paper they called on Zenger, and the first issue of the *New York Weekly Journal* hit the streets on November 5, 1733. The *Journal*'s primary purpose was no secret; it was, wrote Alexander, "(C)hiefly to expose (Crosby) and those ridiculous flatteries with which Mr. Harison loads our other newspaper . . ." Harison referred to Francis Harison, who had effectively been appointed as editor by Crosby himself.

The *Journal* came about in an era when freedom of the press was not assured. Instructions given the governor in 1697 intoned that "For as much as great inconveniences may arise by the liberty of printing within the province of New York, you are to provide all necessary orders that no person keeping any press for printing, nor that any book, pamphlet or other matter whatsoever be printed without your especial leave and consent first obtained." The order had apparently expired by Zenger's time, but the attitude persisted, and those who felt aggrieved at the printed word were quick to go to court.

Zenger, who had little education and struggled with the English language, was not the primary provider of content. That fell to the likes of Alexander and Lewis Morris, a Supreme Court chief justice removed from office by Crosby (as an infant, Morris had inherited the manor Morrisania in the area that is now occupied by public housing in the Southwestern Bronx; his grandson, also Lewis, signed the Declaration of Independence). While Zenger would transcend generations as an icon of a free press, it is not clear that he viewed his role as anything more than a typesetter, and the job as anything more than a paycheck.

But he had to be pleased with the results, for the *Journal* was his first real success. Soon it was running as many as three editions with regular supplements beyond its standard four pages. The writing sparkled with wit and no small amount of snark directed at the sitting governor and his lackeys at the *Gazette*. In the lost and found section, the *Journal* reported that a large lapdog, about five-foot-five, had escaped from its kennel with a mouthful of fanciful plaudits for the governor that it was disgorging at the office of the *Gazette*: "Whoever will strip the said Panegericks of all their Fulsomness and send the beast back to his kennel shall have the Thanks of all honest Men."

In another, Lewis purports to interview a magician who can tell the quality of the governor by the first letter of his last name. The letter "C," needless to say, does not make out so well. Rutherford wrote, "It can readily be seen that the new paper and the radical tone of its articles created great excitement, as nothing like it has before appeared in the Province." Letters to the editor arrived in such quantity that Zenger wrote a notice to his readers, apologizing for not being able to get them all in.

When the governor's libel case against Van Dam came to court, Cosby's hand-picked chief justice, James DeLancey—the man for whom Delancey Street is named—all but ordered the jury to hand up indictments (and simultaneously condemned the "seditious Libels" of the *Journal*) which the jury refused to do, even though the judge made a point to warn "I know most of you Personally." DeLancey's failure, of course, brought catcalls and taunts from the *Journal*. So desperately confounded were the members of the governor's party that they embarked on a clownish reign of terror. A letter arrived at the Alexander house, allegedly written by a pauper, demanding money lest the reputations of the family members be ruined. One and all immediately recognized the handwriting to be that of the *Gazette*'s Harison. In fact, so evident was Harison's hand that Alexander immediately smelled a rat. Perhaps the governor, unable to say for certain who had written unflattering copy concerning his administration, wanted to set a precedent of using handwriting as an admissible form of evidence. Alexander prudently didn't take the bait.

Again and again, Zenger's paper poked the bear, much to the delight of New Yorkers. After a particularly embarrassing defeat for the governor in a magisterial election, the public contributed a couple of raucous ballads of its own. Back in court was the governor, but since the authors of the gleeful songs were unknown, the ballads themselves were indicted and ordered to be burned on the steps of City Hall. One set of papers being laid low, figuratively, at least, the governor's commission next turned its attention to Zenger's *Journal*. A committee ordered that "Zenger's Papers . . . be burnt by the hands of the common Hangman, as containing in them many Things derogatory of the Dignity of His Majesty's Government (and) tending to raise Seditions and Tumults among the People thereof."

It was not going to end well. The angrier the governor got, the more audacious the Morrisites became in print, which made the governor madder still. Crosby notified the mayor and council that Zenger's papers stood accused of stirring up the masses against the general peace and ordered them to attend the public burning. The council not-so-politely declined.

Crosby issued a proclamation against "Ill-minded and Difaffected Perfons," populating the city of New York who were spreading sedition to poison the minds of the King's subjects and "disturb the Publick Peace." He offered a reward of £20 to anyone who would turn over the names of those rabble-rousing songwriters and £50 for information leading the identity of the *Journal*'s columnists, so that they could be brought to justice. The city aldermen, however, said they knew of no law that allowed for meddling with the liberty of the press, and until the governor's people could show them one they had no intention of enforcing any related proclamations. Further, they would not provide the services of the city's Public Hangman or Public Whipper to do the honors of lighting the match—thus the job of incinerating the papers fell to the sheriff's personal slave.

Unable to produce the author of the scandalous documents, Crosby went after the printer himself. Zenger was arrested on November 17, 1734, and imprisoned on unspecified grounds. That Monday the *Journal* did not go to press. Initially denied pen and paper, he eventually was able to write an apology to his readers for missing his publication date, and communicate instructions for the next issue by communicating with his employees through a hole in the jail door. DeLancey set bail at £400, knowing that Zenger's entire net worth didn't come to more than £40. The governor's strategy was to suppress publication of the *Journal* by keeping Zenger in jail indefinitely by setting excessive bail and disbarring any attorney who spoke on his behalf—which is precisely what happened to Alexander and William Smith. To Smith's plea to the court to reduce bail, Chief Justice DeLancey wrote, "You have gained a great Deal of Applause and Popularity by opposing this court; but you have brought it to the point that either we must go from the Bench or you from the Barr. Therefore, we exclude you and Mr. Alexander from the barr."

As power grabs go, this made today's executive orders look like party invitations. In no particular order, the governor of New York had jailed a humble printer under pretenses that had no basis in law; fired a Supreme Court justice; concocted a wild gambit to try to trick his opponents into knotting their own nooses; and disbarred lawyers who were most likely to offer effective defense to his enemies. He might not have been in the same class as Nero, but it had that smell to it.

Crosby and his lackey DeLancey appointed one of their own, John Chambers, to represent Zenger, who had remained imprisoned for the better part of a year, and the race for the future of New York was on. The two sides lined up on August 4, 1735, in the thirty-five-year-old City Hall, still the class of the young city's architecture. Citizens packed the courtroom, understanding that a lot more was on the line than the freedom of a common printer.

From here began an incredible cavalcade of legal parries, with the governor and chief justice on one side, and Smith and Alexander pulling strings behind the scenes on the other, with freedom of the press in the balance. Chambers, floundering somewhat helplessly in the middle, was not entirely the stuffed shirt some had presumed. He asked for a struck jury, which gave both sides an opportunity to eliminate potential jurors they did not like from the pool. The next move was Cosby's. The sheriff dutifully selected the pool from a random drawing of landowners, and lo and behold, a goodly number of men—what were the odds?—turned out to be those who had run for public office on the same ticket as the governor himself.

The next move was up to the Morrisites, who did two things. One, they paid attention to the surnames of the men in the jury pool. As the panel was assembled, their strategy became clear. On the jury were men by the names of van Borsom, Goelet, Rutgers, Hildreth—or, more to the point, men of Dutch ancestry who would not need much of a push to poke a stick into the eye of a British governor.

The second trick of the Morrisites was to secure the services of a better lawyer. They found one in Philadelphia's Andrew Hamilton. Nearly eighty years of age, Hamilton was still mentally sharp, even if bouts of gout made it excruciatingly painful just to get out of bed. His entry into the fray disarmed Crosby, but such was the great lawyer's reputation that even a despotic governor and his chief justice didn't dare disbar him. And really, it would hardly matter who was representing Zenger. It would be child's play to prove that the publisher of the *Journal* "did falsely, seditiously and scandalously print and publish" material that damaged the reputation of the governor of New York.

As there was little argument that the *Journal*'s pages had portrayed Crosby in an unflattering light, the prosecuting attorney reckoned that all he needed to prove was that Zenger physically printed the offending material in order to obtain a guilty verdict. To do so, he dutifully subpoenaed Zenger's employees, who would be forced to testify against their boss. They never took the stand.

Hamilton cheerfully acknowledged that Zenger had overseen the press runs, and instead shifted the focus to one word in the prosecution's case: "falsely." Facing the court, Hamilton said, "I cannot think it proper for me to deny the publication of a complaint, which I think is the right of every free-born subject to make, when the matters so published can be supported by the truth." The implication, of course, was that the columns that ran in Zenger's paper were spot-on: The governor had seized private property for himself; the governor had booted his enemies from the judiciary and replaced them with his friends; the governor had created special courts to suit his purposes. With this, the trial was no longer about Zenger, it was the governor himself who was on trial.

Crosby's men did their best to regain control of the ship. The prosecutor, Richard Bradley, vehemently denied that truth had anything to do with the matter. All that was required to prove libel was to show that the printed material was detrimental to the object of the paper's derision. Matter of fact, the prosecutors said, the libel was even worse if its assertions were true—which, in some twisted way, was probably an accurate assessment. They equated smearing a governor to smearing the king or the Lord himself, to which Hamilton basically said, "Oh stop it." A governor was nothing like a king or a god, and as a matter of fact it was somewhat insulting to kings and gods alike to make the comparison.

Members of the jury were nodding their heads; the prosecution was turning a tad green around the gills. This was not the cut-and-dried affair they had anticipated. DeLancey abruptly cut off Hamilton's request that he be allowed to call witnesses who would verify the truth of the statements in Zenger's paper. He could hardly have done otherwise—to allow a debate over the, as Stephen Colbert would have it, "truthiness" of the *Journal*'s statements would be an admission that truth mattered. But to arbitrarily muzzle the defense effectively lit the fuse on Hamilton's entire arsenal. The governor was a heavy-handed thug, and Zenger's crew had every right to point it out.

Zenger had been imprisoned for eight months, but it took a jury only ten minutes to return a verdict of not guilty. His ultimate acquittal is viewed differently, depending on the profession of those who are doing the viewing. Lawyers say this was not so much a victory of the press, but was instead a victory of the legal system. A tyrannical governor has attacked the judiciary and the bar and had been cut off at the knees. Perhaps they are right. But every journalist knows the story of Peter Zenger and understands that history was made in the New York City Hall in the fall of 1735. It is a fundamental right to speak out against the abuses of authority.

Free speech protections have, of course, expanded since then. They are protected in our Bill of Rights, and in 1960 the Supreme Court affirmed that actual malice is required to prove libel in cases involving public figures. Most journalists will say this is a cornerstone of our democracy, and they will say it began with Peter Zenger.

CHAPTER 3

Botched Abortion, Botched Justice

By all accounts she was a beauty, but because in death she would become a political martyr, the surviving sketches of Alice Bowlsby are most likely somewhat charitable. In one, the railroad stationmaster who discovered her body as it was being checked in for a journey to Chicago is depicted as tenderly removing a lovely, nude, unblemished nymph from a wooden crate. Indeed, according to one account, folds of golden locks cascaded across her bosom as she was pulled from the box into which she had been crammed, her face a vision of "singular loveliness."

The reality was a bit different. Baggage handlers had known something was amiss on the hot August afternoon in 1871 because of the stench.

Alice Bowlsby was in her early 20s with blonde hair and blue eyes, a sweet disposition, and skin of porcelain. By police estimates she had been dead for several days when a shabbily dressed girl booked passage on the Hudson River Railroad to Chicago, along with a trunk that was to accompany her—the plan was, though, only the trunk would make the trip. As a hired cartman, a Jewish peddler boy and the girl herself labored to heave the trunk onto the baggage counter, the clerk remarked that he didn't think the flimsy lock would hold. Did she have a rope, he asked. She didn't, but for one dollar she bought a strap from the cartman, which ought to have been good enough.

Only through the rough handling of the baggage boys— some things never change—did the lid of the cheap trunk happen to split open, releasing a knee-buckling stench of the contents within. Prying open the three-foot trunk, rail authorities found the body of a five-foot-tall woman jammed within, the ghastly freight caked with blood and in the early stages of decay. Nor was her face one of a goddess, the newspapers said, but one grotesquely contorted by the shrieks of pain frozen on her countenance at the time of her death.

Damage to the woman's pelvic area made the cause of death, a botched abortion, fairly apparent, but the identity of the man responsible almost escaped detection. Someone thought he knew the last name of the cartman, and police canvassed the queues of wagons for hire, hoping to find the boy who could lead them to the parcel's place of origin. Several teamsters with a matching name were found, but none had any information about the mysterious trunk. As it turned out, the name had been provided in error, and because of the mistake the perpetrator was oh-so-close to avoiding justice. But at the end of the day, a lad, having heard of the investigation by word of mouth, bravely volunteered to the police that he might be the cartman they wanted, and he led them to the office of a 2nd Avenue physician, of sorts.

The ensuing case would rock the city, which at the time was fervidly against abortion, partially on moralistic grounds, and partially because the standard medicine at the time was such a mess. Even with the best of care, three out of every ten women who received an abortion in New York in the 1870s died. And very few were afforded the best of care. Instead, they were secreted away into the upper floors of hot, grimy townhouses owned by unschooled quacks who fed the women poisonous concoctions or jabbed clumsily away at the fetus with a pointed stick. For this privilege they paid what would today cost them maybe $180. But the abortionists were nothing if not accommodating. They would accept the young ladies' family jewelry, or allow them to pay on credit.

In the genre of back-street abortionists, Jacob Rosenzweig was typical. Had he not gone into abortions, the forty-year-old German Jew might have taken up brewing. His only experience that could even remotely be described as medical, however, was that of a butcher, and it was a fitting description of his subsequent work on frantic women. But he did have a medical degree. In the latter half of the 1800s, the Eclectic Medical College of Philadelphia, for one, was passing them out for today's equivalent of $800. The college dean, John Buchanan (a.k.a., Professor Grind 'em Out) took advantage of the rather remarkable circumstance that few states during the Gilded Age bothered to license their doctors. So, sheepskin in hand, Rosenzweig hung out a shingle—"Ladies cured, with or without medicine"—under the phony name of "Dr. Ascher."

Acting on the cartman's information, police visited the doctor's house. He wasn't there, so they staked out the residence until his return. They eventually saw him ambling down the street and tackled him as he was attempting to purchase a bottle from a neighboring liquor store. The public took an active role in the criminal-justice system in those days, and only by drawing their pistols did the police keep an angry mob from lynching the self-styled doctor on the spot.

That Rosenzweig was the culprit was never seriously in question. But if the police knew who did it, they didn't know to whom he had done it.

Rosenzweig, of course, claimed to have no idea about what the police were talking about, and in court he even denied being an abortionist. A search of the premises turned up little of note, and although news of the horrific event brought forth a cavalcade of tips, they all proved to be dry wells. Everyone with a missing young relative swamped the police headquarters. Then a physician by the name of Theodore Kinne dropped by the morgue and hastily checked the victim's elbow. Fairly sure he knew the identity of the young woman, he visited the 18th precinct stationhouse to talk to the inspector handling the case.

Kinne worked in an office that adjoined Rosenzweig's, and had recently treated a woman fitting the patient's description by the name of Alice Bowlsby. Kinne had noticed a quirky vaccination scar on the young woman that was distinguishable from that of most other doctors. His cursory examination of the corpse revealed a scar on her forearm that matched. Police Inspector Walling was initially disposed to dismiss Kinne as he had dozens of other wild storytellers—but the details provided by the doctor had a ring of credibility. Warren asked Kinne if he could offer any more-substantial proof. Kinne thought for a moment, and asked the detective to give him a day. Then he disappeared.

Enough time elapsed that the inspector decided he'd never see the doctor again. But in the interim, Kinne had rounded up Bowlsby's dentist, Joseph Parker, and led him to the morgue. The attendant wheeled out the coffin and hosed off the body, making it at least marginally approachable. The dentist—recognizing an extraction and two fillings—confirmed Kinne's suspicion, and the two reported their findings to Walling.

The inspector had a name for the deceased, now he just needed to connect it to the abortionist. Hoping to find an article of clothing belonging to Bowlsby, officers turned the house upside down with no success. Then the eyes of Captain Cameron fell on a washtub in the kitchen. He fished around in the gray water and pulled out a handful of garments, including a linen handkerchief bearing some faded lettering that could not be made out under the kitchen's fizzing gaslight. Put under a magnifying glass back at the station, however, police were able to make out the inscription: A.A. BOWLSBY.

Up until this time, Rosenzweig had remained in jail with, the *Times* said, "an air of injured innocence and outraged professional dignity." On hearing of the accumulating evidence, however, this front "had given place to the anxious, careworn bearing of a man in serious difficulty." His wife stopped by for a visit, looking "nothing worse than annoyed," or, as a sergeant put it, "as if she were used to difficult situations."

Confident the noose was tightening, police went back to the Rosenzweig residence, and with the help of newspaper reporters (things were different in those days) gave it a ransacking of a lifetime. This produced a number of meaningful documents, and some others that might have been meaningful, but were not understandable to police, being written in German and Hebrew.

Included in the haul was a stack of blank death certificates and a sheaf of Certificates of Stillbirth and an address book containing the names of sundry undertakers—tools of a doctor, certainly, but not a very successful one. There was more (and why this booty was not discovered in the initial search, the *Times* did not explain). An arsenal of "much-used" abortion tools were evident, as were recipe cards "in cramped penciling, evidently extracts from some evil mentor's fertile brain." By the sounds of the ingredients—nux vomica, iodine, mercury chloride, opium, deadly nightshade, corrosives, sulphuric acid—the *Times* was not exaggerating. Surviving the disease would have been child's play next to surviving the medicine. As Rosenzweig was a former barkeeper, the papers speculated that the bulk of Rosenzweig's knowledge of medicine was learned in a saloon. Perhaps even more tragic was a ledger listing the women who had availed themselves of Rosenzweig's services, and a corresponding column of the men who had shown up to pay for them.

As the case became more publicized, a pattern emerged. It appeared clear that Bowlsby was not the doctor's first victim. Women who died were issued death certificates listing a cause for their demise that belied the trauma he had inflicted. A handshake and a bag of coin were enough to get a friendly undertaker to play along. Other women just disappeared, and were said to have "moved to Europe" or been sent to Minnesota or some other remote outpost for the stated purpose of breathing healthier air.

Following his arrest, Rosenzweig, a portly man with a mousy disposition, spent his time in jail accompanied by newspaper correspondents who dutifully reported on his every visitor and cheered his deteriorating demeanor. Wrote a *Times* reporter, "It was a dismal day for the wretched man, who sat in his cell listening to the pelting rain with a countenance as dark as the lowering heavens without." His manner was described as coarse, and the papers ventured that anyone who had a choice in the matter would never trust his health care to such a thug. The press hammered both the doctor and his chosen discipline, where "the practice of medicine, in his hands, becomes the practice or murder." Reporters gleefully replicated the doctor's accent in print: "These other fellows bromish to do something vot they don't do. I poshitively do all operashunsh widout any danger, and as sheap as anybody." The man claimed to be Russian, but judging by his accent, the papers felt he was more likely German.

The servant girl who had been arrested for her role in shipping the body, seemed, by contrast, rather relieved to be freed from Rosenzweig's shadow. An attractive brunette in her late 20s, Jane Johnson chatted freely with all comers, including the press. She was a country girl who became pregnant and had come to the city to have the child (more likely an abortion, the reporter thought) without her family finding out. She took employment in the doctor's office, she said, to receive care and wages at the same time. But if police assumed she'd quickly turn on the simpering quack, they were disappointed. She denied seeing any young blonde in the office, and only marginally made any references to any sort of trunk.

Still, there seemed sufficient evidence to implicate the abortionist. The cartman identified Rosenzweig as being the man who helped him load the trunk onto his dray, and, while lacking today's science, the link to Alice Bowlsby seemed solid. Rosenzweig was charged with death by medical malpractice, which left many people in the city unsatisfied, including the *Times*, which, editorially, happened to be in the middle of an antiabortion jag. The Bowlsby case became a celebrated cause for the paper, which went so far to obtain the services of a lawyer who explained how the charges could be bumped up to second-degree murder (Bowlsby's jewelry was never found, the lawyer said, indicating that the motive could be seen as larceny.)

The October trial itself focused on manslaughter, but a strong undercurrent of morals was also present. The case "involved not merely the life of two human beings," said District Attorney Samuel Garvin, "but affects the condition of social life and the morals of the entire community."

It would have been unseemly to suggest that the deceased was a loose woman, so prosecutors suggested that she had been the victim of a terrible birth defect—beauty. "Remember," the prosecutor told the jury, "what a struggle these unfortunate girls go through. Born in poverty, and with an inheritance of beauty which is sometimes more ruinous than any gift that could be conferred on them, they are daily tempted by the scoundrels and rascals that surround them."

These unfortunate girls, the prosecution maintained, are flattered, buttered up, caressed, and sorely tempted. The man professes his love and makes her feel like a princess. What can she do? The unfortunate girl falls to temptation, and then

Casanova disappears with no proposal of marriage in the offing. This drives her to the even greater scoundrels who advertise the awful crime that they are willing to perform in the newspapers.

While prosecutors stirred up anger in the jury, the press (successfully) did the same with the public at large. The *Times* reprinted an ad that had run, possibly on the very date that the young woman had died: "Ladies in trouble guaranteed immediate relief, sure and safe; no fees required until perfectly satisfied; elegant rooms and nursing provided. Dr. ASCHER. Amity-place &c." To refute this happy little ad, the *Times* said "The corpse-like faces to be seen peering through the bedroom blinds are enough to horrify the stoutest-hearted passerby."

The *Times* clearly and unabashedly sided with the prosecutors, arguing that the abortionists should be put out of business. "It ought to be done, and a stop put to the wicked career of the monsters who annually expose thousands to the fate of poor Alice Bowlsby," the paper wrote.

Hyperbole aside though, it was much as the paper and prosecutors said. Alice worked in her family's dress shop and was active in her church. She became involved with Walt Conkling, an accountant for a New Jersey silk mill and member of a rather prominent Newark family. He arrived at work the day after Alice's identity had been established to discover his secret was secret no longer, and that he was at the crucible of a raging furnace of malicious gossip. He'd showed up to work without his customary diamond tie pin, and everyone was pretty sure that it was now in the position of the hideous abortionist, payment for services rendered.

Conkling endured a morning of it, and when everyone else had gone to lunch he put a gun to his head and pulled the trigger. To his family, he wrote: "I have long had a morbid idea of the worthlessness of life, and now to be obliged to testify in this affair and cause unpleasantness in my family is more than life is worth. Good by dear father, mother, brother and sister."

Despite the newspapers' contention that the prosecution case was clear-cut, it was not a slam dunk. On the stand, Rosenzweig denied everything. He didn't know Bowlsby, didn't do abortions, and assured everyone that no girl had died in his house from the twenty-third to twenty-eighth of August and that "if she did I would have known about it."

The boy who took receivership of the trunk said he was very sure, then pretty sure, then sort of sure, that Rosenzweig was the man who helped him load. The defense found another woman by the name of Bowlsby to confuse the handkerchief issue, and various scraps of bloody and/or torn clothing police found in the basement of the doctor's house didn't really prove much. Defense attorneys even floated the rather improbable theory that Walt Conklin killed the young woman himself, and then effectively dumped the corpse on Rosenzweig's doorstep and rang the bell. The jury came back after a little more than an hour with a verdict of guilty, but with a recommendation of mercy. The judge ignored the recommendation and sentenced Rosenzweig to the max, seven years of hard labor in Sing Sing.

For Rosenzweig, the future did not look bright. After reading the abortionist the riot act, the judge said he was of the opinion that the crime should have been one of first-degree murder, and that the sentence should have been death. From the bench, he urged the legislature to change the law, which the legislature did—unintentionally, to Rosenzweig's benefit.

Based on a procedural error during the trial, the doctor's attorney had won an appeal, and the right to retrial. As Rosenzweig was awaiting a new trial in the spring of 1872, the New York legislature outlawed abortion, which for the defendant turned out to be a good thing. Since Alice Bowlsby had died prior to the passage of the new law, Rosenzweig of course could not be tried under it. That meant he had to be tried under the old law, which was fine, except that the old law had been repealed by the new, and in the eyes of the law no longer existed. After spending less than a year in prison, Rosenzweig was released. Undeterred by his legal troubles, the doctor returned to the business of mutilating women desperate to end their pregnancies.

CHAPTER 4

The US Mail Underfoot

New York's Chauncey Depew was a true American original who said that the country would have been better off if, instead of the Pilgrims landing on Plymouth Rock, Plymouth Rock had landed on the Pilgrims. Depew was at heart a profit-motivated railroad lawyer—he could hardly have been anything else, although he dabbled in business and loved his two terms in the US Senate and almost made a career of turning down plum government appointments that most men would have drooled over. Bald, with an infectious grin and bushy, snow-white sideburns shaped like hockey sticks, Depew was born in 1834 and educated at Yale and graced the cover of *Time* in 1924 when the magazine sold for fifteen cents.

In both the public and private sector, Depew's services would take (and have taken) volumes to recount. Yet he is best remembered by some as the man who, a century before email, sent the first message in New York by way of an odd yet effective form of rapid communication that for a time transformed the city's postal delivery.

Depew, however, is worthy of a word in his own right. He traveled in, and wrote delightfully about, elevated social circles, including a splendid dinner put on for the Shah of Persia at Stafford House, the finest palace in London, an extravagance owned by the Duke of Sutherland. During the dinner, the Shah leaned over to the Prince of Wales and commented on the fine accommodations. "Is it royal?" he asked the Prince, who replied that it was not, and in fact belonged to a great nobleman. The Shah considered this information and then whispered back, apparently in all seriousness, "Well, let me give you a point. When one of my nobleman subjects gets rich enough to own a palace like this, I cut off his head and take his fortune."

Stories and witticisms were the currency that bought a ticket to the best domestic and international parties the world around. But while Depew was comfortable in the company of the Queen, he was equally at home with the lost souls of the Bowery. One Christmas, a correspondent for the *New York World* asked Depew if he would attend a dinner the paper was putting on "for the tramps who gather between ten and 11 o'clock at the Vienna Restaurant . . . to receive the bread which the restaurant distributes at that hour."

"It was a remarkable assemblage," Depew recalled. "There was among them a representative of almost every department of American life. Every one of the learned professions was represented and many lines of business. Most of them were in this condition because they came to New York to make their way, and had struggled until their funds were exhausted, and then they were ashamed to return home and confess their failure."

The evening was a tremendous success. The combination of a delicious, hot meal, and Depew's deft direction of the affair and his sympathetic and amusing oration caused those in attendance to form a line in the grand hall and demand to shake the Senator's hand.

Depew was quickly and painlessly making his way through the line when an anarchist offered his hand and a confession. The man said he was not himself a tramp, but frequented the lines of men who begged for bread at the Fleischmann's bakery. His mission was to stir up unrest among the crowd, and since Depew was so adept at easing anger and fear, he's come to the dinner to assassinate the Senator that night. "But you are such an infernal good fellow that I have not the heart to do it, so here's my hand," he told Depew.

In fact, Depew seemed to relish hostile crowds. On the campaign trail for one of the many presidential candidates he stumped for, he was approached by some young men from the Bowery who asked him to speak. "The crowd is a tough one, but intelligent, and we think would be receptive of the truth if they could hear it put to them in attractive form," one of the group said. The theater would be packed, if for no other reason than to jeer a dandy with the chutzpah to show his perfumed face in the tough districts famously represented by the Tammany boss "Big Tim" Sullivan. Even Sullivan himself was dubious. He tracked down Depew and said he could not protect him if the crowd turned ugly. Which, the Bowery being the Bowery, it almost immediately did. But Depew had a plan.

He reckoned that poor people resented it more when a wealthy individual dressed down in their presence—a lesson lost on today's presidential candidates who campaign in flannel shirts.

So Depew took the opposite approach, dressing in his finest clothes. It was a plausible theory, but Sullivan had been right—kindness was not in the Bowery's blood, and the audience pounced. "Chauncey thinks he's in Carnegie Hall," bellowed a heckler to the guffaws of the crowd. Another heckler joined in: "Chauncey Depew, you got no business here. You are the president of the New York Central Railroad, ain't you, hey? You are a rich man, ain't you, hey? You don't know us and you can't teach us anything. You had better get out while you can."

Depew protested that he had been born poor, but worked his way up with his own head and hands. "By using them as best I could I have become just what you say I am and have got where you will never arrive." The crowd, if nothing else, appreciated the moxie. A man in a dirty shirt broke the tension by shouting out "Go ahead Chauncey, you're a peach." And for the first time in its history, the district was carried by the Depew's Republicans.

But for all that, it was the peach reference that stuck. The papers had a field day with it, and from that day forward, on American shores or overseas, Depew could never break his association with peaches. A peach even came into play as Depew was introducing what many Americans assumed would be the next big revelation in transit.

Anyone who has ever taken advantage of the outside lane at a branch-bank drive-through has British Isles' inventors George

Medhurst and William Murdoch to thank. Medhurst theorized on the possibility of pneumatic transport around the turn of the nineteenth century. In 1812, Medhurst published a paper exhaustively titled, *Calculations and remarks tending to prove the practicability, effects and advantages of a plan for the rapid conveyance of goods and passengers upon an iron road through a tube of 30 feet in area by the power and velocity of air.* Building on these theories, Murdoch was a Scottish engineer who amassed an astonishing array of inventions in the late 1700s and early 1800s. He might be best known for advances in the steam engine and gas lighting. He is definitely not best known as the inventor of the pneumatic tube, although he performed that service as well (one of his less successful inventions was a steam-powered rifle). In fact, steam engines and gas lights now being a thing of the past, the pneumatic tube might be the Scotsman's invention that has demonstrated the greatest longevity.

Although mostly limited to banking today, pneumatic tubes were not at all uncommon well into the last century. These same familiar bank canisters that are sucked up into a conveyance of tubes to the glassed-in teller once routinely carried interoffice memos or instructions from one floor to another in multistory buildings.

And for a while, they also carried intercity mail. The London Pneumatic Despatch Co. for a decade, used underground tubes propelled by compressed air on a grand scale, employing narrow-gauge rail gondolas three feet in diameter to deliver sacks of mail. But a financial panic and the cars' propensity to become stuck in the tubes doomed the operation.

But America was known to take inventions off European ash heaps and make successes out of them, and in Philadelphia, a more modest version of the pneumatic tube was used to deliver the mail starting in 1893. Postmaster John Wanamaker, who had used the delivery system in his department store, sent the first tube-sent postal message in America. On March 1, he wrapped a Bible in an American flag and sent it from the Chestnut Street Post Office through an underground tube to the Central Office. According to Philadelphia historian Harry Kyriakodis, Wanamaker sent the Scriptures because they represented the greatest message in all humanity—although Mark Twain for one questioned his sincerity, calling Wanamaker an "unco-pious, buttery, Sunday school-slobbering sneak thief." Technology might be better today, but our insults aren't.

Four years later, pneumatic-tube mail delivery came to New York City, and on hand for the dedication was none other than Senator Chauncey Depew, who proclaimed, "This is the age of speed. Everything that makes for speed contributes to happiness and is a distinct gain to civilization. We are ahead of the old countries in almost every respect, but we have been behind in methods of communication within our cities. In New York this condition of communication has hitherto been barbarous. If the Greater New York is to be a success, quick communication is absolutely necessary. I hope this system we have seen tried here today will soon be extended over all the Greater New York."

It was a grand day for the city, the post office being decorated with flags, banners, eagles, and shields. Onlookers had the feeling they were witnessing something special, like Alexander Graham Bell's phone call to Watson, or the launch of a space shuttle. On a grand marquee, the Tubular Dispatch Company posted the delivery times of a message sent from its Tribune Building headquarters and an office at 44 Broad Street. Sent by courier, telegraph, or traditional mail wagon, the message would take anywhere from a half-hour to a little over three hours to arrive. Sent by pneumatic tube, the same message arrived in just four minutes, and thirty-five seconds.

Depew sent New York's first message to travel by subterranean pneumatic tube (the size of which was a little bigger than a man's thigh), a rather unoriginal effort, being a Bible wrapped in an American flag. Depew, however, added a secular touch by including copies of the US Constitution and President William McKinley's inaugural address. The tube traveled the three-quarters of a mile from the city's General Post Office to the Produce Exchange in less than 90 seconds. In three minutes, Depew received a reply—a bouquet of violets. A bundle of mail addressed to Produce Exchange employees went out next. In reply came a basket and note in a flowery hand addressed to "Our Chauncey." In the basket was an oversized, artificial peach, in deference to Depew's celebrated nickname. The crowd of one hundred spectators guffawed, laughter heartily joined by Depew.

Then, like kids with a new toy, men sent the tubes flying back and forth: clothes, papers, food, and, inevitably perhaps, a sack containing a live, tortoise-shell cat. The hilarity that ensued among the bureaucrats when someone came up with the idea of stuffing a cat into the tube must have been considerable, as they anticipated the reaction on the other end. If anyone considered the poor animal's survivability, the concern was overridden by the gag. "How it could live after being shot at terrific speed from Station P in the Produce Exchange Building, making several turns before reaching Broadway and Park Row, I cannot conceive, but it did," wrote postal supervisor Howard Wallace Connelly in his autobiography. "It seemed to be dazed for a minute or two but started to run and was quickly secured and placed in a basket that had been provided for that purpose."

But the cat got people to thinking. If the animal could survive rapid transit beneath city streets in a pneumatic tube, could not a human being survive as well? And other tube-related schemes were popping up in rapid succession. The city post offices would be connected; then every home would have its own private connection, much like today's electrical wires; then mail would fly in tubes from city to city. Think of it. No more lumbering, horse-drawn wagons or trains that could only travel where the tracks took them. For a couple of decades, the pneumatic tube technology seemed as limitless and futuristic as beaming people from a planet surface to the Starship Enterprise. And, as these things go, everyone was falling all over each other to achieve first-mover status on any number of projects, some legitimate, some hair-brained, but all relatively amusing.

A prototype pneumatic subway had actually predated the success of the mail tube by two decades. An American inventor, Alfred Beach, took the pneumatic tube to the next level, proposing to build a subway powered by compressed air. Beach had become absorbed with the problem of congestion on Manhattan streets. Streetcars, carriages, wagons, and pedestrians clogged the main avenue with volume similar to what is seen today. A subway was an obvious solution, but finding a satisfactory method of propulsion was a problem. Horse-drawn carriages were inelegant, and steam engines belched out smoke and soot that, in a tunnel, had nowhere to go but into the eyes and lungs of passengers.

Pneumatic tube theory developed by the Brits projected that objects could be propelled by compressed air at speeds of up to sixty miles an hour, and as they were limiting their experiments to relatively small parcels, Beach didn't see why full-sized rail cars wouldn't work equally well—speedily transporting people underground without steam or horse. Beach unveiled a prototype at the 1867 American Institute Fair. A gleaming, wooden tube six feet in diameter and twenty feet long ran between 14th and 15th streets, and delighted participants in groups of ten boarded a car and were whisked the length of the pipe in just a few seconds.

Beach correctly calculated that the public would be enchanted, and he reckoned he could parley this excitement into support for a pneumatic subway. Beach incorrectly gauged the opposition of one William M. "Boss" Tweed, who at the time was comfortably accepting kickbacks from the trolley company that certainly stood to lose considerable business if a subway proved successful. Tweed was not about to allow for any subterranean competition, and effectively blocked Beach from receiving the necessary permits. Stonewalled by Tweed, the exasperated Beach went back to the drawing board.

Still intent on putting pneumatics to use in one way or another, he returned to City Hall and asked for a franchise to build a subterranean mail system, which would whisk letters and packages well beneath the above-ground melee. To this, the city willingly agreed, and Beach, accompanied by his son and a few trusted employees, commenced to tunneling. For two years, Beach's project inched forward, accessed through the basement of a haberdashery at the corner of Broadway and Warren. As the weeks and months went by, most people forgot all about the postal project. Beach attracted little attention, working underground and hauling away the excavated earth at night. He went so far as to wrap the wagon wheels in fabric, so as not to disturb people as they slept.

Then early in 1870, the city's most prominent dignitaries received a curious invitation. Their presence was desired at the corner of Broadway and Warren—not above ground, but below it. It was a bewildering request that was all but impossible to ignore. When the guests descended a stairway beneath the basement of Delvin's Clothing Store, there were no words to express their astonishment. The passage opened up into a bright, luxurious hall that, wrote Julia Solis in her book *New York Underground: The Anatomy of a City*, was of "legendary opulence" and "resembled the luxurious sitting room of a grand mansion." The gushing newspaper reports compared it favorably to Aladdin's carpeted cave.

Soft strains of music rose from the keys of a baby grand piano. Chandeliers illuminated a fountain and a tank filled with goldfish. Paintings hung on the walls, and velvet curtains mimicked window dressings to ease the fears of any claustrophobics who might be in attendance. The unveiling created the intended uproar, both among the people and in the press, who could have been excused for thinking they were witnessing the next great innovation in a great city.

Needless to say, this was not a waiting room designed for the comfort of some ink-stained postmaster. Every last stitch in the velvet upholstery was designed to impress the public and give New York politicians no choice but to move forward with the city's first subway. Along with the shock and awe, it was a stick in the eye of Tammany Hall. In perfect secrecy, not a block from the city offices where Boss Tweed customarily parked his graft-riddled keister, Beach had built not a mail tube, but a short, working stretch of pneumatic subway.

At the end of the luxurious hall, a cylindrical rail car was waiting to give the invited guests the ride of a lifetime. Twenty people at a time nestled into the plush seats of the carriage. A one-hundred horsepower engine powered a gigantic fan, which built up enough air pressure to move the car. It scarcely reached ten miles an hour before it had to begin slowing down in the short pipe, but the public was enthralled. It was motion without noise, soot, or manure. "The ride became as popular with the public as Coney Island's shoot the chutes," wrote the *New York Times*.

Again, Beach relied on public support to overpower Tweed's grip on transportation, and again he was disappointed. Beach was correct that the public would demand relief from the congested streets, but failed to appreciate Tweed's ability to counterpunch—not to mention the friends the Boss had in high places. Seeking to bypass the city bureaucracy, Beach headed to Albany with a $5 million subway proposal only to have Tweed head him off at the pass with an $80 million plan for a network of elevated trains. There was little question whose project New York's Boss-friendly governor would support.

Still, Beach persevered. For three years, New Yorkers lined up to pay twenty-five cents for the brief ride, which made up in novelty what it lacked in length. But his hopes of eventually prevailing in the state assembly never panned out. With

Tweed in the background, the New York legislature refused to grant Beach permission to expand his project. Even Tweed's removal from office on corruption charges failed to help. The governor, contending that Beach had violated the terms of his franchise, ordered the attraction to be closed in 1873, and the once-promising enterprise was walled up.

Although Beach envisioned his wind-powered subway serving all of Manhattan and beyond, other engineers weren't so sure that the technology was viable over so extensive a project. And whatever glimmer of hope remained, it was extinguished by the Panic of 1873, which crippled much of the world for the better part of a decade and dried up the capital that such an endeavor would have required. Beach died in 1896, but his ghost received a brief renaissance seventeen years later, when a crew excavating for a stretch of city subway—finally becoming a reality in 1912—smacked into an odd obstruction. Punching through thr brick, they discovered the entombed pneumatic subway, its rail car decayed, but the tunnel otherwise in tact.

If the pneumatic subway had a melancholy end, the future of pneumatic mail was brighter; the irony is that had Beach proceeded with plans for a pneumatic mail system, as he had represented to City Hall, his reward might have been considerably greater. At the General Post Office, after the levity of Depew's peach, cats, etc., died down, the benefits of the mail system became apparent. Or so people thought.

Pneumatic mail delivery survived in New York City for more than half a century, much in the way that ethanol has survived—partly on its merits and partly on its press clippings, but mainly because once the private tube companies got their clutches into lucrative federal contracts, their army of lobby-ists made sure that the gravy train remained on the tracks.

The tubes were genuinely useful and efficient for a time. The canisters, two feet in length, flew through the tubes as if they had "been shot from a popgun," the papers said. The loop of nine-inch, cast iron tubes, buried several feet beneath city streets, ran from Battery Park to Harlem and then back down through Times Square and Grand Central Terminal. Cross-city tubes ran across the width of the city and eventually reached Brooklyn at present-day Cadman Plaza by pig-gybacking on the Brooklyn Bridge. At its height, 55 percent of the city's mail was carried in pneumatic tubes, traveling beneath the city at thirty miles an hour. (Curves slowed them down; in a straight line, the tubes would have been capable of speeds approaching 100 mph.) Power stations with electric motors and blowers pumped compressed air into the tubes. The skilled operators who fed the canisters into the tubes were known as Rocketeers.

The routes covered twenty-seven miles and connected twenty-three post offices, and were unaffected by the winter-time ice and snow that could paralyze traditional mail carriers. After a blizzard in 1914, supporters crowed that businesses that had availed themselves of the tubes received their mail without delay, while wagons above ground were tied up for days. Trying to broaden their territory, tube companies backed John Henry-like contests in which taxicabs filled with missives and merchandise raced against the tubes—and lost, as a gen-eral thing. The federal Post Office Department sent postmas-ters from western cities to witness the pneumatic mail-tube systems employed in Philadelphia, New York, and Boston, and federally appointed commissions at the turn of the twentieth century were enthusiastic. Tube lines were eventually dug in St. Louis and Chicago as well, and at its height, each tube delivering two hundred thousand pieces of mail each hour.

But despite the plaudits, there were problems, most notably the cost. The government leased the tubes from private companies, an amount that in 1917 had reached $17,000 a mile. Even a decade prior, government auditors were becoming wary of the costs. A federal report in 1907 by the US Postal Inspector concluded that the tubes were "the most expensive method of mail transportation in use at the present time, and the Inspectors very much doubt whether the advantages obtained are commensurate with the heavy expense." Multiple times, Congress appeared ready to pull the plug, but despite several suspensions in service (including World War I) tube-company lobbyists generally prevailed in the end.

One of the more entertaining stories of legislative shenanigans occurred in Albany in 1897 when the New York Parcel Dispatch Company was seeking approval of legislation for a contract to lay tubes beneath the streets of New York and the Hudson River. As was often the case in these matters, the contract seemed far too sweet, and a number of lawmakers, including an assemblyman by the name of Patrick Trainor, were opposed. The bill passed the Senate, and when it arrived in the lower house a curious thing happened. A man approached Trainor and asked if he might like to meet a handful of attractive actresses who were engaged at a local theater. This seemed like a fine idea to Trainor, and he went off with the actresses who were skilled at acting as if they were dazzled by everything the assemblyman had to say.

At the same time, a second staunch opponent of the bill was lured out of the chamber on the offer of a free cigar. Other opponents were distracted in similar ways. In the ongoing buzz of the chamber, somehow no one noticed that the bill had come up for a vote and—without its primary enemies present—it passed with little notice. "Then everyone woke up," wrote the *New York Times*. "Mr. Trainor left the entertaining group of actresses, and hurrying to the clerk's desk demanded a copy of the role-call and for the balance of the session was in a rage."

Along with the prohibitive cost, it was more common than was convenient for the system to break or tubes to become stuck somewhere under the streets of New York—at which point a major construction project was required to retrieve the wayward canister. Grease had to be pumped into the tubes to keep the canisters sliding efficiently, and seeing as how oil and paper don't mix, anytime a canister would rupture, the Postal Service would be left with a wad of unsalvageable paper; what could transport letters six hundred at a time could occasionally destroy them six hundred at a time.

But in the end, the mail tubes became an anachronistic mole on the government beast, allowed to exist only because removing it was more trouble than it was worth. The several thousand letters still being transported by tube in the early 1950s were an eyelash compared to the fifteen million outgoing and twelve million incoming letters the New York Post Office was handling each week. Letters that went by tube could easily be tossed on one of the city's many mail trucks at virtually no added cost.

The federal government temporarily suspended the mail-tube service on December 1, 1953, and a month later the suspension became permanent. Few people noticed, because even at the time few New Yorkers realized that as they walked the city streets, the US mail was whizzing along beneath their feet. Pneumatic tubes did still remain in use for a time as a memo-delivery system in multistory buildings. Some lasted long enough to be finally put out of business by email and the PDF—missives whose speed would have delighted Chauncey Depew.

CHAPTER 5

The Grand Slave Conspiracy that Wasn't

The New York winter of 1740–41 had been horrific. Matters were already looking dicey by the fall when much of the harvest was ruined by two weeks of cold, soaking rains. Frigid weather set in a month earlier than normal, and throughout the winter the snow was relentless. Horses, cattle, and sheep died in massive snowbanks. Three feet remained on the ground in March, and winter conditions lasted through April. The price of corn doubled and by winter's end it was not to be had at any price; money at this point was useless, and even the wealthy were forced to beg for food. As spring approached, everyone was hungry, exhausted, and more than a little edgy.

The poor, or course, had it worse. Among their numbers would have been both black and white—New York had more slaves in the mid-eighteenth century than any North American city, save Charleston, South Carolina. Added to these unfortunates were indentured servants, whose lot in life was little better, their one bright spot being the light of freedom at the end of a years-long tunnel.

Northerners liked to tell their slaves that they were better off than slaves in Southern states. Slaves digested this news with much the same skepticism as a child who has been told that starving children in Third World nations would be thrilled to have mayonnaise on a saltine cracker for an after-school snack. In a sense these Northern slaveholders were correct; conditions in the steamy fields of the Deep South were exhausting, particularly in comparison with the Upper South and North, where the work was often more domestic in nature.

Still, as in the South, the white population was always nervous about the potential for slave revolts. Many times these fears were founded upon rumor and baseless hysteria, but not always. In 1712, a New York slave named Kofi set fire to his master's outhouse. When a group of townsfolk arrived to put out the fire, Kofi and his followers pounced—nine men were killed and six injured. If Northerners felt they were more benevolent toward their slaves under normal circumstances, all that supposed enlightenment went right up the flume in the wake of violent revolts. Twenty-one slaves were quickly executed for their role in the 1712 uprising in all manner of gruesome ways.

Thirty years later, the memory of Kofi's revolt might not have been fresh, but slaveholders certainly would have known about it. Certainly too would they have been keenly aware of more recent slave revolts in the South, including the infamous

Stono Rebellion two years prior. There, a literate slave referred to as Cato, led eighty of his fellows in a march toward St. Augustine in Florida, where the Spanish, in a thinly disguised effort to undermine British authority, had promised the slaves freedom and land of their own. The small army of slaves killed twenty-one whites before being subdued by the South Carolina militia. In the aftermath, forty-four slaves were killed or executed and South Carolina passed legislation making it illegal to educate a slave.

And to add to the tension in New York, the British had gone to war with Spain in 1739—a conflict known as "The War of Jenkin's Ear"—and Manhattanites were pretty sure that the enemy would recruit "Spanish Negroes" in New York to sabotage British interests.

So with all this as context, New Yorkers were ready to believe in anything that walked, talked, and quacked like a conspiracy. It was, in fact, a slave by the name of Quack who set the events in motion, even though, when all was said and done, no one could say for sure that the New York Slave Revolt of 1741 actually happened. It might have been, in no particular order, a pure rebellion in which slaves attempted to cast off their bonds; an uprising of the lower class regardless of race in protest of their miserable plight; a plot hatched in conjunction with the Spanish; or, nothing at all. Hecklers from Boston accused panicked New Yorkers of enacting their own version of the Salem witch trials. And, because old records were lost in subsequent fires, there is only one primary source that records events of the time. But like too many primary sources, this one is primarily flawed, in that the author, city recorder Daniel Horsmanden, was principally concerned with protecting the reputation of the city's investigation. Of course the investigation was real enough, and so were the executions that came of it.

Also real was a fire that broke out on a blustery March day at the governor's house in Fort George at the southern tip of Manhattan Island. The lieutenant governor had ordered a plumber to repair a leak in a gutter that connected the house to a nearby chapel, and it was initially supposed that the wind blew sparks from the pot of coals the worker carried with him to keep his solder iron hot, igniting the roof. The problem, it was later concluded, was that the fire appeared to start not on the roof, but under it. And in several different places. This was enough evidence to rule out the smoking solder gun as the culprit—at least in retrospect, when townsfolk were barking up a far more sinister tree.

Arson, it was now believed, was the cause, and it was easy to see why attitudes changed so quickly. Because in a week's time, fires were breaking out right and left, at a couple of homes, a warehouse and a stable. In a neighborhood of some considerable wealth, a pile of glowing coals was discovered in a haymow and extinguished by a passing pedestrian. In an era of wood homes and wood heat, fires were common enough. But to a number of people frazzled by the long winter, this seemed like something more.

The city council called for an investigation, and turned the matter over to Horsmanden, who piggybacked it onto an existing investigation of theft that was focusing its suspicions on a handful of Spanish slaves. Into this situation, wittingly or unwittingly, stepped Quack, who was walking up Broadway on the Sabbath to church with a couple of fellow slaves, when a resident, Mrs. Earle, swore she heard him chant "Fire, fire, scorch, scorch, a little dammit, by and by."

Whether Quack was placing a curse upon the city or muttering some singsong nonsense to himself was impossible to tell, but Mrs. Earl, for one, wasn't taking any chances. On learning his name, she passed it along to her local alderman who notified the council as a whole and it resulted in an escalation of the judicial proceedings. An entire cottage industry fixated with parsing the true meaning of Quack's words broke out in the city. Mrs. Earl added the detail that after his utterance, Quack raised his hands skyward and laughed, which added a whole new dimension to the vignette. Some thought that Quack was rejoicing at public unrest over the fires. Others thought he was saying that the fires to date were just the tip of the iceberg, and that by and by a greater conflagration would present itself.

That translation seemed plausible on April 6, when four more fires broke out, two in the neighborhood of a newly acquired Spanish Negro disgruntled by his recent sale into slavery. Even as slaves were helping to put out the fires, white residents looked at them askance, trying to determine whether they were really helping, or just pretending to. Just as one fire was being contained, another cry of fire rang through the streets. Flames were just beginning to shoot out of a wooden warehouse, when a passerby spotted a slave, who dropped from an upstairs window and sprinted into the streets. The onlooker shouted "A negro, a negro!" a cry that was caught and repeated by the crowds, who bastardized the fact of one negro running into "The negroes are rising!" Horsmanden later wrote on the "terrible apprehension" in the city at that point. The slave who started it all was quickly apprehended and carried (literally) off to jail, but so too were a number of slaves whose only offense was of the wrong-place, wrong-time variety.

Naturally, all eyes turned to Quack at this point, as the one person who seemed to have insight into the proceedings. Pressed, Quack admitted to uttering the words in question, but assigned them an entirely different meaning. Quack said he was merely celebrating the recent naval victory of Edward Vernon, who with Lawrence Washington (George's brother) at his side, had just captured a Spanish stronghold. If true, Quack wouldn't have been the only one to be impressed with Vernon's accomplishment—Washington went so far as to name his estate Mt. Vernon after the British officer.

But to a majority of the people present at the time, Quack's explanation sounded like a reach. Horsmanden concluded that the fires were the result of "some villainous confederacy of latent enemies among us." The board of inquiry didn't know the motive of this confederacy, but it intended to find out. Any white person who solved the riddle would be given the reward of £100, and a free black or Indian would be awarded £45. Any slave who came forward with information would be freed and awarded £20, with his master compensated for the loss. The militia was called out, homes in the affected communities were searched and passersby were subjected to an examination of their parcels—all eerily similar to today's terrorism precautions.

An inquiry began on the morning of April 21, the purpose "to present all conspiracies, combinations, and other treasons down to trespasses (regarding) the many frights and terrors which the good people of this city have of late been put into, by repeated and unusual fires." Among the impaneled jurors were a couple of men who had lost buildings to the unusual fires and were unlikely to be in the market for not-guilty verdicts.

It was at this point that Horsmanden's initial theft investigation took on added relevance. In the 1730s, a cobbler named John Hughson had moved south out of Yonkers, and opened a seedy tavern on the Hudson waterfront. It soon became a crossroads for slaves, free blacks, poor whites, and riffraff in general. It also became known as something of a colonial yard sale for stolen goods, and two weeks before the first of the fires broke out, Hughson had been arrested for trafficking in ill-gotten property. Specifically, he was accused of dealing with two slaves suspected of theft who went by the names of Caesar and Prince, who had recently been fingered as the culprits in a city dry-goods shop robbery. In the dank circles of the waterfront, Caesar and Prince were part of an underground ring known as the Geneva Club, a name derived from a brand of Dutch gin that was a frequent mark for the thieves.

The ring had proved hard to crack until Horsmanden coerced a young indentured servant named Mary Burton into testifying against Hughson. But she didn't stop there. With freedom from indenture as a welcome alternative to prison, the sixteen-year-old girl readily swore that the Geneva Club met at the tavern not just to launder stolen goods, but to conspire with white ruffians to burn down the city. She also implicated Hughson's wife Sarah and Caesar's Irish girlfriend, a prostitute who went by the name of Peggy Kerry, and was supposedly the mother of Caesar's child. She said that thirty or so slaves would meet up at the tavern on Sundays to drink, shoot dice, and go over details of the plot. When all the elite, white people were dead, Hughson would assume the role of King of New York, with Caesar his Vice King. At this point, Burton's word was all that Horsmanden had, but for him it was enough. Robbery and arson had intersected on the waterfront of the Hudson.

The theft-ring trials began on May 1, and it took less than a day for the jury to convict Caesar and Prince of robbery. On May 2, they were condemned to hang, but not before receiving a somewhat disjointed lecture from Judge Philips about how fortunate they had been to be tried and sentenced to death in the same manner than any white villain would have been. The judge also went on to say that he was pretty sure the two had done a lot of other bad stuff for which they had not been punished "for by your general characters you have been very wicked fellows (and) hardened sinners." There was one small glimmer of hope, the judge continued, that the Almighty might go easy on them in the next life if they turned states evidence against others involved in the plot. If any of this impressed Prince and Caesar it didn't show. Both went to the gallows on May 11 unrepentant and with lips sealed. A disappointed Horsmanden noted that they "died very stubbornly." But as Caesar's gibbeted corpse twisted lazily in the breeze, everyone else with an ax to grind or a neck to preserve was pointing fingers right and left. The jails were literally filled with suspects as no slaves, particularly those with Spanish ties, were above suspicion.

Meanwhile, even as testimony was set to proceed in the case against John Hughson, Hughson's wife Sarah and Peggy Kerry, now dubbed the "Newfoundland Irish beauty," fire broke out in seven barns. Two blacks who happened to be caught in the neighborhood were summarily burned at the stake. Conspiracy or no, the white population was panicking, and the spring of 1741 had taken an ugly turn. Now becoming more convinced of a connection between burglary and arson, the tavern owner's trial was postponed until further investigation could be completed.

With the public desperate for answers, Horsmanden's ears pricked when another Hughson servant named Arthur Price revealed to him that Peggy Kerry had mentioned something about an arson conspiracy that involved the Hughsons and multiple slaves, including Caesar, Prince, and Cuffee. The judge threw Price, Cuffee, and a bottle of rum together in the same cell, and before long Cuffee confided in Price that the cur who burned down the governor's mansion was none other than Quack.

Horsmanden was all too eager to believe Burton's story of a mixed-race conspiracy, which played into his long-held belief that nothing good came of whites selling spirits to blacks. As word of the reward money got out, more poor wretches came forward to talk, and as they did, more properties burned to the ground—with even more people coming forward to say they knew who did it. Two confessions independent of Horsmanden's account survive, one being that of an Indian slave who said that Hughson would swear slaves to secrecy lest "Thunder and lightning might strike him dead and the devil fetch him." Then he would outline the plot, urging them to burn their masters' homes, at which point they "were to have what white women they pleased, and that each Negro was to take his master's gun" and meet up later to conquer the burning city.

Likewise, a New York slave said he was witness to Hughson & Co. attempting to rally "as many negroes as they could" to assist the French and Spaniards. One other colorful detail depicts the men sitting around that tavern sharpening their knives "to cut the white men's heads off."

Evidence of the plot seemed to be gaining steam and Quack and Cuffee were next to feel the effects. Whether those standing trial were guilty or not, by now there was little in the way of a criminal proceeding to give them any protection from a bloodthirsty citizenry. The court accepted the testimony of a nearsighted man who was only able to "distinguish colors" who placed Cuffee at the scene, over the testimony of several eye-witnesses who said the slave was at his master's, sawing wood and mending sails. Quack had alibis as well, but it hardly mattered. The jury believed the government's assertion that the two proposed to "establish themselves in peace and freedom in the plundered wealth of their slaughtered masters." The fellows received another one of the court's patronizing speeches, being reminded that "your lot is superior to that of thousands of white people. You are furnished with all the necessaries of life, meat, drink, and clothing, without care, in a much better manner than you could provide for yourselves, were you at liberty." Fighting fire with fire, Horsmanden ordered the pair to be burned at the stake; as they neared the wooden poles to which they would be tied and saw the heaps of kindling on which they were to stand, both roundly confessed and implicated a number of fellow slaves. They were wasting their breath. No one was in the mood for charity, and as the executioners readied the site, a considerable crowd chided them for taking too long to light the match.

Nor would this change when the accused white co-conspirators stood trial in June 4. This, for the townsfolk, was the main attraction, since it was hardly thought that a black person was capable of orchestrating such a complex event. The morning of the trial, Hughson asked to see the judges. Horsmanden granted him an audience, but before the accused could speak, the recorder reminded Hughson of his "wicked life," assuring him of his guilt on all charges and that he and his family were headed to the gallows. This was before the trial, mind you, but in his assessment of the situation Horsmanden proved to be prophetic. The prosecutor went after Hughson guns blazing, calling him, for starters, a "grand incendiary" and an "arch rebel." Fearful, perhaps that he wasn't getting his point across, he went on to call the barkeep the "devil incarnate," "Geryon of darkness" and, saving his best work for last, "chief agent of the old Abbadon of the infernal pit."

Contrary to the judge's earlier lecture to Caesar and Prince, the white defendants did indeed have some rights that black defendants were not afforded. For example, they were allowed to strike names from the jury pool, which they did, taking care to ensure that none of Peggy's past clients wound up on the panel—no small task, by the sounds of it. Still, they faced an uphill, probably impossible battle, given the mood of the town and the hefty bonuses that witnesses stood to make in exchange for their testimony. The young servant Mary Burton was an early witness; she would later collect her £100 pound reward and be freed of her indenture. It's hard to say she didn't earn it. She effectively testified against her masters to the point that the Hughson family (according to Horsmanden's account) began weeping and embracing each other and crying out over the injustice of her betrayal, considering that they had cared for Mary and taught her to read the Bible and fear the Lord, just as they had their own children. These demon-strations must have lost some of their luster when, upon hear-ing Mary testify that Hughson had sworn negroes to secrecy on the Bible, Mrs. Hughson jumped to her feed and said she could prove the girl was lying, "for we never had a Bible in the world." In need of a plan B at that point, Mrs. Hughson called for her infant who suckled at her breast until the court ordered the demonstration to cease.

If the testimony against the Hughson's and Peggy Kerry was compromised, the testimony offered in their defense was likewise not terribly convincing. A couple of defense witnesses toed the Hughson line, but a third—perhaps having not been properly briefed—acknowledged seeing "whole companies of negroes" shooting dice at the tavern.

From the bench, Harsmanden declared the four guilty, so it was of little surprise that the jury did the same. The Hughsons and Peggy Kerry went to the gallows on June 12 (daughter Sarah's execution was delayed in hope she might talk), but none confessed.

With the ringleaders thus disposed of, the courts now turned their attention to mop-up duty, rounding up any and all who might in any way have perpetuated the plot. Six more slaves were sentenced to death in early June, but one, Jack, agreed to confess in exchange for his life. This led to another roundup of fresh suspects, and more confessions led to more arrests until it began to dawn on the public at large that some were more interested in saving their own skin than in seeing justice done. That same thought crossed the mind of Daniel Horsmanden, but at this point he could hardly cast doubt on the process, at least not openly.

Yet even the lieutenant governor believed the trials and executions—before the summer ended there would be thirty-one in all—had gotten out of hand. One or two executions, he felt, might have been enough to get the point across. Indeed, forty-two blacks were pardoned just to bring some sanity to the situation. Which it almost did, but not in time to save the life of a short white man who stood accused of being a Catholic priest (a capital offense in New York at the time). John Ury claimed he was merely a teacher of Latin and Greek, but to the court he was the source of oaths, incantations, and other "bloody hocus pocus" that set the negroes on their fiery pursuit. Whenever the prosecution felt its hand weakening, it reached for the Mary Burton card, and the girl turned in a star performance, swearing that Ury was knee deep in the occult arts, with crucifixes and charred babies as props. Sarah Hughson was pardoned just in time to take the stand and testify that Ury was in charge of absolving the negroes from any sin they might commit.

Ury was hanged on August 29, an event the city used to declare an end to the open season on arsonists. Three weeks later they celebrated a day of thanksgiving for all their good work in getting to the root of the conspiracy, which it appears they did—and then some. In retrospect, it seems likely that the rapid succession of fires was not an accident, but that they may have been more in response to isolated injustices on the part of slave owners. Quack, for example, had motive because his wife was a slave at the governor's mansion, where he was prohibited from seeing her. It also seems clear that the Hughsons sold liquor to slaves, facilitated gambling and prostitution, and employed a stable of petty thieves. Less likely is that John Hughson had any idea of burning down the town and naming himself king.

It is also unlikely that all those who were executed were guilty—the greater possibility is that a sizable majority of them weren't. Many refused to confess even when faced with being burned at the stake. And many of their accusers were simply aiming to avoid sharing the same fate. Much of the entire case for the plot as the public perceived it seems to have rested on the shoulders of the young indentured servant, Mary Burton. Without her, the case against the Hughsons, Peggy Kerry, and John Ury was paper thin, and without the guilt of these principals, the whole conspiracy to overthrow the government angle would have faltered as well—at least in the eyes of colonial New Yorkers who felt that slaves were incapable of complex thought. Mary had no interest in testifying until she was threatened with imprisonment and tempted with freedom and a healthy reward. A year after the city's celebration the council paid off her indenture and awarded her the remaining £81. She was never heard from by history again.

CHAPTER 6

Mark Twain Takes New York by Storm and Spirit

For the great American author Mark Twain, New York City was a second and sometimes first home. It was a city with which he had reached an uneasy truce. New York, he wrote, "is a splendid desert—a domed and steepled solitude, where the stranger is lonely in the midst of a million of his race. A man walks his tedious miles through the same interminable street every day, elbowing his way through a buzzing multitude of men, yet never seeing a familiar face, and never seeing a strange one the second time. Every man seems to feel that he has got the duties of two lifetimes to accomplish in one, and so he rushes, rushes, rushes, and never has time to be companionable—never has any time at his disposal to fool away on matters which do not involve dollars and duty and business."

Yet New York provided Twain with the thing he loved most: material to write about. He appeared to equally enjoy New York and enjoy insulting New York. Whatever, New Yorkers clearly loved him for it. And, when in New York, Twain did more than write about his grievances, he leapt in with both feet, taking on rude trolley conductors and Tammany Hall with equal vigor. In his book *Mark Twain: Unsanctified Newspaper Reporter,* James Edward Caron made note of this contradictory nature, which led to love-hate relationships. Watching daily the agonizingly slow construction of a pedestrian bridge over a busy New York City street, Twain browbeat the workers for their lack of speed and itched for the day the infrastructure would be available for public use—until it did in fact open, at which point he was no longer interested in using it.

Twain said he found it impossible to hold his temper in New York. Congestion and rudeness he found on city streets completely exhausted his arsenal of profanity: "You do not swear anymore now, of course, because you can't find any words that are long enough or strong enough to fit the case," he wrote.

A quarter century after Twain's death, President Franklin D. Roosevelt gave a speech dedicating the Mark Twain Bridge over the Mississippi River, telling the great pleasure it had given him as a boy to shake Mark Twain's hand. He then went on to wax nostalgic over Twain's glorification of the American boy through the lives of the adventurously naughty Tom Sawyer and Huck Finn: "With every American who has ever been a boy, I thrill today at this great structure joining two states in the commemoration of youths immortal."

But as a man of contradictions, while Twain might have celebrated boys in literature, in real life he was more judicious.

As he aged, boys, particularly New York boys, were as convenient a target as anyone else. When a street urchin filched his umbrella, Twain offered $50 to anyone with information that would bring the boy to justice, but $200 for anyone who would "bring me his remains."

Twain spent several years in New York that were quintessentially Twainish, grousing not just about bridges and boys, but all manner of things and acting out in ways that had his neighbors nervously asking, "he's joking, right?" although no one was ever sure. He did his best to reform New Yorkers in any way he could, such as a letter to the editor of the *New York Sun* to voice his disapproval of conductors' behavior on the city's horse-drawn trollies. In recounting his poor treatment on the trolley, he suggested that, while city folk were accustomed to such rudeness, "us hayseed folk from the back settlements . . . are so delicate, so sensitive—well, you would never be able to imagine what it is like."

On this particular day, Twain boarded the car with three ladies who, like Twain, were forced to stand in the aisle. "Of course there was no seat—there never is: New Yorkers do not require a seat, but only permission to stand up and look meek, and be thankful for such little rags of privilege as the good horse-car company may choose to allow them." Worse, Twain and the three ladies in question happened to be standing in the way of the conductor who wanted to get through and take tickets. The conductor "took me by the lapel and said to me with that winning courtesy and politeness which New Yorkers are so accustomed to: 'Jesus Christ! what you want to load up the door for? Git back here out of the way!'"

Twain explained that he was not accustomed to being spoken to in such a manner, and he would appreciate it if the conductor would not swear in front of the ladies who, by their own cowering reaction, Twain took to be country people as well. Whatever tools the conductor had in his own personal skill set, customer service was not among them. Flummoxed, he did the only thing he could think of—he offered Twain a plug of tobacco. This was the wrong answer, for Twain took his badge number and headed to the trolley's main office to file a complaint, "but there was nobody in the superintendent's office who seemed to want to converse with me. A man with 'conductor' on his cap said it wouldn't be any use to try to see the president at that time of day, and intimated by his manner, not his words, that people with complaints were not popular there, any way."

And when words didn't work, Twain was not above going to court. In November 1900, he pressed charges against a cabbie who overcharged and insulted him. Twain, by this time, was an international sensation, and the courtroom was packed with onlookers awaiting the punchline. The *Times* reported that "The people who witnessed the trial were wondering all the time whether it was another of Mark Twain's jokes, and they expected to hear him tell a funny story about how he wept over the tomb of Adam, 'my original ancestor.'"

But Twain was dead serious. Instead, it was the court itself that became a comedy, with press and spectators jammed into the small space and a throng outside the doors. Clerks, clearly enjoying the moment, cracked jokes over the bizarre scene, while the judge, clearly not enjoying the moment, sweated profusely and tried to accommodate the celebrity in his midst.

With Twain presenting his own case, it became apparent that the cabbie had charged him $1.50 for a $1 fare, an event that most people in that time and place would have found to be relatively normal.

For Twain, this made the people of New York complacent in the crime. When the owner of the cab company complained that a piddling little overcharge was not worthy of such a media circus, or for that matter even a complaint, Twain could hardly contain himself.

"I am doing this just as any citizen who is worthy of the name of a citizen should do," he said. "Here is a man who is a perfectly natural product of an infamous system. It is a charge on the lax patriotism in this city of New York that this thing can exist. You have encouraged him in every way you know how to overcharge. He is not the criminal here at all. The criminal is the citizens of New York who have encouraged him."

No one knew exactly what to make of this. Finally the cabbie decided, foolishly, perhaps, to speak a word in his defense. "We stand for hours at a time without a fare, and you can't blame us if we make it up when we get one," he said. Twain replied that this was a great argument if one happened to be a pirate. Before the situation could escalate, the judge quickly ruled for the suspension of the cabbie's license and adjourned the hearing. As the onlookers filed out, he wiped his brow and said "What a damned fool that cabbie was."

The next day, the papers sang that "Mark Twain Is Avenged," and ran playful stories about the great cab caper. For Twain, it would not be his last win in what proved to be a very short stay.

Twain made New York his home for a little more than a year in 1900, when he was in his mid-sixties, living in a brownstone at 14 West 10th Street in the fashionable Washington Square neighborhood. At the height of his popularity, he thrilled people who happened to glimpse him walking city streets, and packed any venue at which he chose to speak. At the New York Press Club there "gathered together such a crowd as the newspapermen had never seen in their clubrooms before," the *New York Times* reported. At political rallies he packed theaters, with men standing in window casings and any other place they might find a toehold, and straining from the streets to catch a word or two of Twain's caustic and influential speeches.

Twain's turn-of-the-century intersection with New York arrived at a time when the city was at a political crossroads. Through most of the preceding century, the city had remained in the grip of Tammany Hall, a political machine that had its roots in a social order established in 1786. In the late 1700s, a network of Tammany Societies popped up throughout the cities of post-Revolution America. The name was a derivation of Tamanend, an Indian chief in the Delaware Valley who was revered for promoting peace among the Native Americans and Europeans. Sadly, his view of international relations did not prevail, but his name did—although not in a way the great chief might have appreciated.

By 1800, the Tammany Society in New York had begun to swim in political waters. Such was its growing influence that, led by soon-to-be-Vice President Aaron Burr, it denied John Adams the state's electoral votes, costing him reelection and awarding the presidency to Thomas Jefferson. The corruption for which Tammany became known was fast in coming, not that other factions in the city were immune to patronage and graft. By the middle of the century, Tammany had consolidated its power on the shoulders of thousands of immigrants driven to America by the Irish potato famine. Tammany Hall at it's most infamous was under the control of William "Boss" Tweed who, if one could overlook the crime, vice and corruption, ran an admirably tight ship. Progressive projects and programs took root. The Boss protected his people and they rewarded him with their votes. The more honest and upright members of the city only lost their patience with him when he failed to control warring Irish factions in the Orange Riots of 1870–71. But if Tweed didn't survive (he died in prison), Tammany did, and no matter who did what to the pull the plug on the machine it always lived to fight another day. It had not, however, had to reckon with Mark Twain.

The mayoral election of 1901 pitted the reformer Seth Low against Tammany's Edward M. Shephard. In the background, however, loomed the boss Richard Croker who did an outstanding job maintaining and adding to Tammany's reputation for corruption. Low benefited not just from Twain, but from an upstart group no one had ever heard of that called itself the Order of the Acorns. The Acorns were the brainchild of a handsome, curly-haired newspaper reporter named Joseph Johnson Jr., who worked for William Randolph Hearst at the *New York World*. It was part of a "Fusion" ticket, so named because it was a coalition of Tammany's enemies, whose past fragmentation had helped the machine stay in power.

In particular, the Acorns sought to weed out corruption in the police force. In a statement of purpose, the Acorns declared that they "Will have much to say concerning the present administrative weaknesses, but they propose dealing especially with the city police now smelling to high heaven.

The Order will not be persuaded to drop this issue. No devil may turn monk before this November."

If Twain would publicly call out a rude trolley conductor and take a price-gouging hack driver to court, he could certainly be counted upon to lead the charge against a corrupt bureaucracy.

Unlike today, the campaigns formally began one month before election. Twain had sworn he would not speak during the campaign, a vow he was unable to keep—he got around this by "reading" his speeches instead of speaking them. In a particularly effective address to the Acorns at the Waldorf Astoria, Twain read Edmund Burke's indictment of the corrupt governor of India, Warren Hastings, substituting Croker's name for Hastings: "The crimes of Mr. (Croker) . . . were crimes not against forms, but against those eternal laws of justice which are our rule and our birthright." For the comic Twain, this was serious stuff. His introduction of the Irish hero Burke was not accidental, of course, in a city full of Irish immigrants.

The speech went viral, published in a supplement of *Harper's Weekly*, and reprinted as a pamphlet by the hundreds of thousands. The week before the election, Twain appeared in public again, not in a somber meeting place of a private club, but in a grand public hall on Broadway. "A crowd of more than 2,000 jammed into the place," reported the *Times*, "and was so thick that several times the management had to interrupt the speakers to prevent surging, and injury to many people in the audience." When the doors opened a stampede of humanity all but carried away the police officers whose job was to maintain order. "Within the hall every available inch of space was called into requisition," wrote the *Times*. "Men and boys climbed up the latticework surrounding the elevator at one side of the hall, and climbed up onto window sills and wherever there was an inch to give a foothold above the heads of the rest of the men." It was, said political operatives, the largest and liveliest crowd ever to witness such an event; one and all had come to see the Fusion candidate Low, but more to see Twain "throw bombs of humor into the camp of Tammany."

At five minutes until noon, Twain, accompanied by Johnson and Low, waded through the thousand or so who had failed to get a seat and then into the hall and up onto the stage. This would be no serious, scholarly dissection of Burke. Twain said he had deep respect for Shepard, but compared the Tammany mayoral candidate to one good spot on an otherwise rotten banana. And no matter how acceptable that little white spot on a rotten banana might be, the whole fruit ultimately had to be tossed. Which is exactly what the voters of New York City did, handing the victory to Low and ending the rein of Tammany as it was then understood. The machine did survive—as a reform party, of all things—but without the boss Corker, who resigned his leadership post and headed back to the British Isles.

But in 1901, largely with the assistance of Twain, the dragon had been slain and the slayers were in the mood for a party. It took the form of a parade that began on Broadway and ran uptown with only a slight idea of where it would end up. Croker had derisively referred to the acorns as the "popcorns," so those leading the parade made sure to deviate from the route to go past Tammany headquarters. The hall appeared to be mostly deserted with the exception of secretary Thomas F. Smith, who, the papers noted gleefully, was "peering furtively" from behind a curtain. Twain was the hero of the day, and he rose to deliver a eulogy for the "dear departed" Tammany Hall. An estimated crowd of five thousand people enjoyed the day, barely escaping what nearly became a melee between the Fusion supporters and the Tammany-controlled police.

In front of the Metropolitan Opera House, the celebrants burned Croker in effigy, an insult that almost precipitated a riot. The police pulled their billy clubs and charged the perpetrators, but at that moment someone in the crowd yelled "Three cheers for Mark Twain," and the ensuing roar splintered the phalanx of police like a soprano shattering a wine glass.

The prop of the day was a broom representing the sweeping of Tammany's influence from office. Brooms decorated windows and doors and were carried by the parade marchers like regimental rifles. Hats and coats of the men on stage were festooned with miniature brooms, and patriotic music filled the air as dignitaries prepared to speak. Twain was not especially humble in a victory that Low won by thirty thousand votes. "I am not surprised at the superb majority we had," he told a crowd that erupted with every statement. "What surprises me is that Tammany got a single vote . . . but while a thirty thousand majority was not nearly large enough, we will not quarrel with Tammany about the result. Tammany is dead and it is no use to quarrel with a corpse."

Twain saved some of his best lines for the defeated individuals of Tammany, including Asa Bird Gardiner, a corrupt district attorney who was removed from office by Governor Teddy Roosevelt and who had famously remarked, "To hell with reform." To which Twain responded, "Well, reform has been started in the way indicated and we do not care how soon he goes the same way."

Tammany's losses were financial as well as political, in an age when the Wall Street financial district facilitated action in elections as well as industrials. The 1901 election attracted wagers totaling more than a half million dollars. A Tammany syndicate apparently failed to see the handwriting on the wall, and it cost them $300,000.

As mayor, Seth Low did what he promised to do, replacing patronage with a merit-based civil service system, reforming the police department, improving educational opportunities—but, as always, the idea of reform proved to be more popular than reform itself, and Low was voted out of office after one term, losing to George McClellan Jr., son of the Union Civil War general.

Twain would still have plenty to say, and he spent the last decade of his life as he had in that year in New York in 1901, trading in the hilarious, rawboned stories of his early career for "a pen warmed up in hell" pointed against whatever injustice caught his attention. But even in death, his spirit lived on in New York—at least this was said to be the case at his 14 West 10th Street brownstone, which has become rather unglamorously known as the "House of Death" for its plethora of spirits, including Twain's. Witnesses say he's appeared in his classic white suit sitting in the ground-floor living room or descending the stairs. (If Twain's ghost had wanted to be historically accurate it would not have appeared in white, a look Twain didn't adopt until 1906.)

The ghost stories likely would not have stuck save for two relatively modern events. In 1957, an unremarkable actress Jan

Bryant Bartell took up residence in the former Twain home, and starting seeing spirits from the get-go. The first was "a monstrous moving shadow Loom(ing) up behind," and it was pretty much downhill from there. Tim Donnelly reported in the *New York Post*, "The incident took several minutes, and several cigarettes, cups of tea and nips of brandy to shake off. But it wouldn't be the last in the seven-year stretch of psychological and sometimes physical torment Bartell suffered from what she claimed were the icy hands of the house's former inhabitants, reaching out from the afterlife to grab her."

She turned these dalliances with the dead into a 1974 book, *Spindrift: Spray from a Psychic Sea*, that she did not live to see through to publication—she died in 1973, either of suicide (according to police) or a heart attack (according to her publisher). Her supporters saw her as a sympathetic figure, a talented but troubled soul who struggled to figure out what or who tormented her.

Twain's house, once an iconic and celebrated residence, became miserably known for tragedies—it's been reported that twenty-two people died within its walls, including a six-year-old girl who was beaten to death in 1987 by her adopted father, in a case that made international headlines.

These events revived interest in the specter of Twain and the time he spent in New York City. In the only record of his ghost speaking, Twain, sitting near a first-floor window said to a woman and her daughter, "My name is Clemens, and I has a problem here I gotta settle." Then he disappeared. New York did give him plenty of problems, but he seemed adept at settling them himself.

Chapter 7

The Rise and Fall of Little Germany

The middle of the 1800s was an unsettled time for Germany, in no little part because there was no Germany as such, but a collection of thirty-nine German states that were about to be wracked by one revolution after another. Seeing the handwriting on the wall, many of the sovereigns in these states assumed they were goners and headed for the hills, only to discover to their astonishment/relief that the liberal forces behind these revolutionary movements were quite incapable of governing, and basically collapsed under the weight of their own ineptitude.

But the issues that led to the revolutions in the first place remained, even if the likes of Karl Marx and Friedrich Engels were unable to fully take advantage of them. The standard of living to which the skilled workers in greater Germany had become accustomed was declining, particularly due to the textile technology that was coming online in Britain. Land was not available in sufficient quantity to support the growing number of individual farmers, and the violent century made it more likely that young men would be drafted into an army. Crop failures were all the more acutely felt by farmers who had no margin for error and by artisans who grew no food at all. One account, retold in Stanley Nadel's *Little Germany; Ethnicity, Religion and Class in New York City*, 1845–80, was of an apprentice locksmith named Frederick Bultman, who as a thirteen-year-old boy was on his way to pay his father's taxes when he was passed by a gilded, royal coach. It struck him at that moment just whose money had paid for the carriage's gold decorations, and he immediately resolved to escape to America, a land that was better known at the time as *kein König da*, or "no king there."

The final push came about with the advent of the steamship and cheap transport. People who wanted to get out of their country could now afford to do so. Steamboats reached deep into the interior rivers, offering a first step to, hopefully, a better life. Those who left didn't all go to America, but many did, and while not all the German immigrants to America settled in New York, many did that as well. Germans through the decades left for New York, sometimes in trickles and sometimes in waves, building up the German population in the Lower East Side until it was a city within a city. By the end of the century, New York's Little Germany neighborhood represented the third largest Germanic city in the world, behind only Berlin and Vienna.

This city within a city, however, wouldn't last. And ironically, the same vehicle that transported men and women out of Germany was instrumental in its rapid demise, when a horrific steamboat accident wiped out a broad swath of Little Germany's population and demoralized those who were left.

The Germans called the community *Kleindeutschland*; the Irish called it Dutchtown. As recently as 1800, it had been little more than salty marshland, part of a farm owned by the peg-legged Dutch founding father of New York, Peter Stuyvesant. The area had been drained in the early 1800s, a move that benefited both developers and the government that collected tax on development.

The sizable enclave in the Lower East Side represented a relatively large fraction of the hundreds of thousands of German immigrants to America in the second half of the nineteenth century. They filled up the Lower East Side, but filtered out to other parts of the city as well. German influence was everywhere, as the city's beverage of choice began to transform from Irish whiskey to German beer. Consisting of four hundred blocks and as many as one hundred fifty thousand people, Little Germany—bordered by the East River in the east and the Bowery to the west—was a self contained explosion of life. Throughout the neighborhoods were beer gardens, concert halls, beer gardens, theaters, beer gardens, libraries, beer gardens, churches, and even beer gardens. A virtual cottage industry arose of the German proclivity to shun classical theater and symphonies in favor of a tankard of lager and an oom-pah band. German singers at the time were compared, and not favorably, to a particularly rough millstone. One social critic noted they would skimp on newspapers, opera houses, and lecture halls, while spending $120,000 on a beer hall. But what beer halls they were, grand affairs capable of holding more than one thousand people at a time. When the weather was hot these became outdoor recreation centers, whose music and laughter filled the streets. The other popular pursuit in summer was steamboat excursions to local harbors or promontories for picnics and festivals. It would be one of these outings that would prove to be the downfall of Little Germany.

Immigrants at the time were typically unskilled and prone to vice, but not the residents of Little Germany, most of whom knew a trade and were industrious. Of all the immigrant groups, the Germans are perhaps the only group that has not been featured in a movie about organized crime. They made clothes and shoes, crafted fine musical instruments, rolled cigars, joined furniture, baked bread, brewed beer and peddled dry goods.

"The immigrants did not merely enter the economy as isolated individuals," Nadel wrote. "They colonized it. At first, Germans dominated a few trades, then many trades, entire industries and even whole sectors of the economy became German in character."

At the street level were the storefronts, with residential space upstairs and a small factory or workshop in the basement or in the interior of the block. German attitudes toward labor sowed the seeds of future labor unions, and by the second half of the nineteenth century, German political influence was sufficient to elect hand-picked candidates to the offices of mayor and Congress.

The soul of the community might have been Thompson's Square, a ten-acre park known as much for political movements as playgrounds. On January 13, 1873, in the midst of a financial panic and depression, seven thousand unemployed workers, including twelve hundred from Little Germany held a protest there, which was brutally quashed by police. Less violent but even more devastating to the German artisans was the Industrial Revolution, which introduced machines that increased productivity, but also drove down wages. To make the same money, it became necessary to work longer hours, and work more frantically. Needless to say, this new, harried way of life was a far cry from the old, slower, artisan way. And many German immigrants were not happy with the change. Factories grew larger, bosses grew meaner, and conditions deteriorated. Even children felt the change, as "reformers" concluded that the best way to get an urchin off of the street was to put him on a factory floor. Twelve years of age, it was felt, was not too soon to begin developing a strong work ethic.

By the 1880s, a number of forces were beginning to strain the ties that bound the previously tight-knit community. Class conflicts became more open, pitting the increasingly exploited factory workers against the increasingly elite capitalists. Businesses that had once operated as families now operated as corporations. Labor unrest swirled, often violently, amidst economic panics that further battered the old way of life. Many of the wealthier people who lived in *Kleindeutschland* began to drift to the nicer Upper East Side community of Yorkville, and their numbers were not replenished, as German immigrants found the post-war Homestead Act a tempting opportunity to own a meaningful chunk of land in the nation's interior, with very few strings attached.

Yet it was one final, tragic blow that devastated the social fabric of Little Germany, and spelled the end for a community that was already in decline.

Six weeks before the final voyage of the steamship *General Slocum*, city officials inspected the boat's lifeboats, floatation devices, and fire-fighting equipment, and pronounced it all to be in fine shape. First rate, no problems at all. As it would turn out, this wasn't exactly true, but inspectors in those days didn't trouble themselves with things like dry rot and rust. Nor was there any consternation that the lifeboats were more or less bolted to the gunwales, rendering them useless in an emergency. Besides, nothing on the order of what was about to happen had ever happened before, so there was little inclination but to keep the money conscious owners of the Knickerbocker Steamship Co. happy.

The keel was laid for the *Slocum* in 1891, and it was named in honor of Gen. Henry Slocum, a competent if plodding commander of New York infantry in the Civil War. After the war he was elected to Congress and later was appointed to head the Brooklyn city works department, where he helped facilitate the Brooklyn Bridge. His floating namesake, however, was nothing to be quite so proud of. It stumbled and bumbled around Manhattan Island like a drunken sailor, running into sand bars and bouncing off of other ships with startling regularity. On one memorable excursion, nine hundred liquored-up anarchists lived up to their name by trying to take over the boat. At nearly the length of a football field and capable of carrying three thousand people or more, it was not agile. Nor was the crew agile at handling emergencies—it was lacking in even the most basic of disaster training, having not performed so much as a fire drill.

Indeed, the *SS Slocum* bore strong resemblance to today's Third World ferries that are little more than floating cattle pens. But the Knickerbocker ships at least looked nice—all freshly painted and neat and tidy above decks to give the illusion of a ship-shape operation. But in places the public was never allowed to see, a time bomb was ticking.

The dual-sidewheel, three-deck steamer was a popular excursion boat, rented out for $350 (nearly $10,000 in 1904, or about $5 a ticket) to haul up to three thousand passengers to popular parks and picnic destinations. The traffic was virtually nonstop in the summer, as New York residents evacuated hot city streets for the cool shorelines. On June 15, 1904, the *Slocum* was booked by the St. Mark's Lutheran Church on Sixth Street in Little Germany for a daytrip to a Long Island park at Eatons Neck. It was to be quite a celebration, the end of the Sunday School year, and more than fourteen hundred passengers, mostly women and children were excitedly looking forward to a day of games, food, and laughter. With flags flying and a band playing a snappy tune, the ship left the East Third Street pier at 9:30 in the morning and headed up the East River bound for Hell Gate and Long Island Sound. For a half hour, everything seemed normal, witnesses told the *New York Times*: "With no thought of the coming disaster, no effort was made to keep any of the parties together, and the children ran happily all over the ship, while the mothers gathered on the upper decks and gossiped. They were nearly all German women, who knew each other, and had something in common to talk about."

But beneath the bow of the steamer was a lamp room, where the ship's lighting fixtures were topped off with oil. Straw soaked up the oil that was inevitably spilled on the floor, and piled of rags were on hand to clean the lamps. The miracle was that nothing bad had come to pass on a prior voyage. On this day luck ran out, and a stray match or cigar butt ignited the lamp-room straw. At least that was one story. Another blames an exploding stove that was being used to simmer a pot of chowder. Whatever, a young boy noticed the smoke and tried to warn the crew, but his cries went unheeded. It wasn't until smoke began to pour from the bow that the crew realized the boy had been telling the truth. Another ten minutes went by before the captain, an old man with forty years experience named William H. Van Schaick knew what was going on. By then it was too late.

Fire seemed to burst from multiple points on the ship at once. Rooms that held varnish and gasoline exploded in flames. The new season's coat of fresh paint looked nice, but was also highly combustible. The poorly trained crew had little idea how to fight the blaze; they at least were able to hook up the fire hoses and turn the water valve, only to have the dry-rotted canvass burst under pressure. His ship fast becoming an inferno, Captain Van Schaick had a decision to make. Horrified onlookers cried out from the riverbank, trying to attract the captain's attention and encourage him to beach the craft on the shoreline a hundred yards away. Instead, Van Schaick opened up the throttles and aimed for North Brother Island, still perhaps a mile away. The papers said he "lost his head."

The captain later said, with some justification, that he feared holding tanks filled with fuel on riverbank would explode had the flaming ship plowed into them. If that were true, it would have been only slightly worse than what was to come.

Panic spread through the passengers as fast as the flames, which were fanned to new heights by the speeding steamer.

The screams of the women and children mixed with the roar of the boilers and the mammoth, twelve-foot piston arm that powered the twin paddle wheels. The *New York Times* painted a grim picture: "The scenes attendant upon the disaster have seared themselves in the brains of the survivors never to be effaced. Women were roasted to death in sight of their husbands and children, and babes by the score perished in the waters of the East River, into which they had been thrown by frenzied mothers. With death by fire behind them, hundreds leaped to their doom in the river."

Few were able to swim, not unusual for the time, and even those who could were weighed down by layers of woolen clothing. Women grabbed for life jackets, some of which—unused and, for all intents and purposes, uninspected over the past dozen years—crumbled to dust in their hands. Those life vests that held together were actually more dangerous. The story went around that the manufacturer, in order to make the floatation devices seem more substantial than they actually were, had sewn iron rods into vests, and filled them with cheap, but ineffective cork. Women wrapped their children in the vests and lowered them onto the water, only to see them swallowed beneath the surface.

The disaster played out within plain sight of the city, whose residents acted nobly to do what they could. Other boats in the river hauled in what survivors they could find, but soon found themselves engulfed in a sea of floating corpses, most of them women and children. From the shore, watermen and factory workers risked their own lives to try to swim out into the river and pull in survivors. By this time, the forward half of the ship was ablaze, with the wind blowing the fire inexorably toward the huddled masses in the stern. The *Times* wrote, "With sure death from fire behind, the women waited until the flames were upon them, until they felt their flesh blister, before they took the alternative of the river. Babies shrieking with pain, many of them with their clothes on fire, were dropped into the water by scores, and finally the women were forced over the rail and hundreds of them fell into the river."

Van Schaick did manage to get what was left of the ship to the island, but, even there, sound judgment failed him. Instead of landing on a beach or pier, he put the boat aground on a rocky section of shoreline that made rescue all the more difficult. On North Brother Island at the time was an old smallpox hospital that was serving as an institution for those suffering from infectious diseases. Nurses and patients alike raced to the scene and heroically did what they could. Perhaps the most amazing, and successful, rescue effort was put forth by the crew of the tugboat *Wade*, which had been tied to the North Brother Island pier. With amazement and horror, the crew watched the blazing *Slocum* steaming toward them at a top speed. As the *Slocum* neared, the crew of the *Wade* cast off, timed it as best they could and pulled even with the doomed ship just as she was hitting shore. At that precise moment, the badly charred timbers holding the upper decks gave way, and the planking collapsed in shower of sparks, flame, and human-ity. The jolt literally catapulted dozens of women and children, their clothing in flames, onto the deck of the *Wade*, where deckhands extinguished them fast as they could. All told, the papers credited the crew of the *Wade* with saving 155 people.

Another story of outstanding heroism soon made the rounds. Policeman Thomas Cooney of the East 88th Street station, answered an emergency call to the island. From their tug, the men of the *Wade* watched as Cooney swam out to rescue a drowning passenger. Then another, and another. In all they saw him pull eleven people to shore. He was on his way for the twelfth when, overcome by fatigue, he himself slipped beneath the surface, never to come up.

If the conflagration itself was chaos, the aftermath was nearly as bad. Thousands of people, friends and family from Little Germany and well-wishers and the curious alike, descended on the shoreline and on the morgues that were called on to do a job for which they were never intended. In all, 1,021 people were dead. Macabre scenes played out across the city, where every wagon that was available was pressed into hearse duty. Row after row of corpses lines shorelines, morgues, and police stations. One little girl was discovered unscathed amid a pile of bodies. After watching her mother burn to death, she spent the night in a police station that was doing double duty as a makeshift morgue. She spent the night staring at the rows of bodies and wailing "Momma is all burned up" in between her sobs. A six-year-old boy arrived at Lincoln Hospital hugging a hobby horse—he'd jumped off the flaming boat clutching his toy, and it apparently had enough buoyancy to keep him afloat until he was rescued, displaying nary a scratch.

For the community of Little Germany, it was the end. Damage had been done that could never be repaired. The memories were too harsh. Children lost their parents. Parents lost three, four, five children. "Whole families have been wiped out," wrote the *Times*. "In many instances a father is left to grieve alone for wife and children, and there was hardly a home in the parish, whence but a few hours before a laughing happy crowd went on its holiday, that was not in deep mourning last night."

Almost overnight, the thousands of people who had lived in *Kleindeutschland* disappeared. Many moved uptown or into new neighborhoods, until only a relative handful of German families remained, and the Lower East Side became home to newly arrived Jews and Eastern Europeans. In 1940, St. Marks was converted into a synagogue.

The *Slocum* tragedy, the city's worst loss of life until 9/11, did move the federal government to tighten steamship regulations, but outside of that the only person to pay any price at all was Captain Van Schaick, who was sentenced to ten years for criminal negligence and failure to maintain proper fire safeguards. He served three and a half years before being pardoned by President Taft. The steamship company paid a nominal fine, despite pretty strong evidence that it had falsified safety records. Other agents of the company were indicted but not convicted. As the captain was taken from the courtroom, he told reporters, "Boys, I was the victim of circumstances. I tried to do my duty as I saw it. I think my sentence was pretty harsh for an old man, but I have no fault or criticism to make."

The last survivor of the disaster, Adella Wotherspoon, died in 2004 at the age of one hundred, having been an infant at the time of the fire. The last living survivor who remembered it was Catherine Uhlmyer Connelly. At the time of the wreck, she was eleven, and recalled seeing people drown in the waters of Hell Gate and being killed when they jumped and hit the paddlewheel. In an interview in 1989 when she was ninety-six she said, "Sometimes he is very cruel, the man upstairs." She died in 2002 at the age of 109.

CHAPTER 8

New York's Cross-Dressing Governor

To be considered the worst governor ever appointed to an American colony took some real work. Very few came to these shores intent on becoming a beacon of good government and if they were accomplished in the administrative arts, they would have lived a far more comfortable existence meting out policy in their native land. Some of the colonial governors worked out better than others, and could point with relative pride to their accomplishments.

But probably the majority came clutching some get-rich-quick scheme to their breasts—they would, in their minds, make a quick fortune in the colonies before scurrying back across the sea to civilization. Needless to say, those who failed at home seldom fashioned a successful second act in America. Stupidity, corruption, brutishness, and incompetence were common. Colonists in the main were aching to push deeper into the wilderness and acquire new lands, but to do this they needed some semblance of governmental help. Over and over they would appeal for more favorable land policies, trading assistance and protection from the Indians but, unless it had the potential for a healthy payoff, their governors seldom seemed interested in affairs beyond their own courtyards. Several armed conflicts broke out prior to the Revolution, as colonists tried to get their governors to do their jobs.

But if there is an award for the worst of the worst, it might go to Edward Hyde, 3rd Earl of Clarendon, Lord Cornbury, who served as governor of New York and New Jersey from 1701 to 1708. Lord Cornbury was a joyous sort, the type of man who was self-assured enough to dress up in women's clothing and hide in the bushes along a New York street, pouncing on unsuspecting passersby, cackling with laughter at their all-too-predictable response. While it seems wrong to criticize such wholesale enthusiasm, many people did, and in an age when an ill-advised text message can cost a politician his job, the mystery is how he was able to last for six years.

Some of the stories surrounding Lord Cornbury have been debunked, but then some of the debunking has itself been debunked in a battle of historians that has roots in both sides of the Atlantic and involves the identity of the subject and sexuality of a three hundred-year-old painting. But either way it's an intriguing piece of history—one that is either about the debauchery of an early public official, or the depths to which his enemies would sink in their quest to remove an innocent man from office. In these matters, the safest course is often to assume that the truth is somewhere in the middle.

Robert Emmet Odlum was a swimming instructor who grew bored with distance swimming and turned to high jumping. On May 19, 1885, he raised his arm in the air for balance and leaped from the Brooklyn Bridge. It did not end well. *Courtesy Frank Leslie's Illustrated Newspaper.*

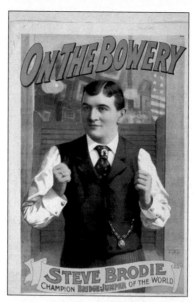

Steve Brodie might or might not have jumped from the Brooklyn Bridge. But he parlayed the story into a great career as a showman that included several theatrical productions. *Courtesy Library of Congress.*

"By no means," exclaimed Hamilton, in his clear, thrilling, silvery voice. "It is not the bar, printing and publishing of a paper that will make it a libel: the words themselves must be libelous, that is, false, scandalous, and seditious, else my client is not guilty." Page 558

The aging attorney Andrew Hamilton was a ringer obtained by the enemies of New York's corrupt governor to defend printer Peter Zenger against charges of libel. "By no means," exclaimed Hamilton, in his clear, thrilling, silvery voice, "Is it the bar, printing and publishing of a paper that will make it a libel: the words themselves must be libelous, that is, false, scandalous and seditious, else my client is not guilty." *Courtesy Library of Congress.*

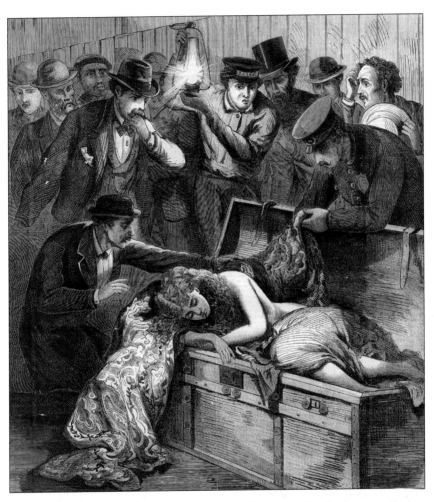

Alice Bowlsby was probably not in this great a shape when her body was pulled from a flimsy trunk being shipped to Chicago. The victim of a botched abortion, her case became a sensation, but did not result in justice. *Courtesy © Chronicle/ Alamy Stock Photo.*

A brilliant statesman, Chauncey Depew believed in American ingenuity and sent the first piece of mail delivered in New York City by an underground, pneumatic tube. He received a peach in return. *Courtesy Library of Congress.*

A *New York Tribune* sketch of the machinery that propelled the mail by pneumatic tube. Industry lobbyists kept the system alive long after it had outlived its usefulness. *Courtesy Library of Congress.*

Daniel Horsmanden led the charge to put down a rebellion of slaves and lower class whites. By the end, however, even he seemed to understand that the conspiracy might have been less than the sum of its parts.

Fear swept through New York in 1741 after several suspicious fires. The judicial system fought fire with fire, burning suspects at the stake.

For Mark Twain, New York was a second home. He became involved in city politics and at the turn of the twentieth century led the reform ticket to victory. *Courtesy Library of Congress.*

The *General Slocum* steamship disaster spelled the end of Little Germany's glory days. Those who escaped the flames by jumping into the water fared no better in the end, because few people at that time and place knew how to swim. *Courtesy The Mariners' Museum, Newport News, Va.*

Portrait of an Unidentified Woman, unidentified artist, ca. 1700–1725. Some believe this is not a woman at all, but Lord Cornbury, New York's (allegedly) cross-dressing governor. *Courtesy New York Historical Society, Photography © New York Historical Society.*

British actor William Charles Macready unwittingly triggered a massacre when he introduced a bit of song and dance to the Shakespearean tragedy *Hamlet*. *Courtesy National Portrait Gallery, London. Used by permission.*

An American rock star, actor Edwin Forrest's blue-collar fans took great offense to any suggestion that their hero was in any way inferior to European actors. *Courtesy Library of Congress.*

US troops were called in to quell a riot outside of a New York theater. No one dreamed they would be ordered to open fire, particularly those innocent bystanders who were only there to watch the fun. *Courtesy The New York Public Library Digital Collections.*

A 1798 watercolor of the Collect Pond. Bayard's Mount, a 110-foot hillock, is in the left foreground. Prior to being leveled around 1811, it was located near the current intersection of Mott and Grand Streets, Manhattan. New York City, which then extended to a stockade that ran approximately north-southeast from today's Chambers Street and Broadway, is visible beyond the southern shore. *Courtesy Metropolitan Museum of Art.*

Some credit promoter Tex Rickard with inventing the concept of the modern day superstar. He was also the founder of the New York Rangers and built the third incarnation of Madison Square Garden. *Courtesy Library of Congress.*

Isidor and Ida Straus were on the maiden voyage of the *Titanic*. The Macy's Department Store magnate declined to leave the ship before all the women and children had been saved; Ida declined to leave him. *Courtesy encyclopedia-titanica.org.*

An iconic part of Woodlawn Cemetery, the Belmont mausoleum, patterned after DaVinci's Saint-Hubert Chapel in France, is the final resting place of Oliver Hazard Belmont, whose family founded the Belmont Stakes. Here, he is joined by his wife Alva Vanderbilt Belmont in 1933, one of several prominent suffragists resting at Woodlawn. She was interred with a banner proclaiming, "Failure is Impossible." *Courtesy Library of Congress.*

New York's architectural preservation movement came a hair too late to save George Post's best work, the massive New York Produce Exchange. The 1884 colossus was one of the most important buildings in America at a time when agriculture was king. *Courtesy Library of Congress.*

Castle Garden on the left is a detail from "The Bay and Harbor of New York" by Samuel Waugh (1814–1885), depicting the castle in 1848. Before Ellis Island, this was where immigrants, welcome and otherwise, entered America. *Courtesy Museum of the City of New York.*

Elizabeth Cochran Seaman, a.k.a. Nellie Bly, gained fame for circumnavigating the globe. But her more important work came as an investigative journalist. *Courtesy Library of Congress.*

THE POLICE, UNDER THE DIRECTION OF INSPECTOR DOWNING, CLEARING THE PIGGERIES OF BERNARD RILEY.

City residents' habit of raising hogs became a victim of gentrification, as no one strolling through the new Central Park wanted to be assaulted by squeals and smells.

Probation ended the trade of liquor on American shores, but not in international waters. A fleet of ships, including the rumrunner *Surf* shown here passing by the Statue of Liberty, hung off the US coast selling hooch to small vessels that would sneak it ashore. *Courtesy National Archives.*

What's known is that Edward Hyde was born in southern England in late November 1661, with plenty of familial
earls, barons, and viscounts for company. Most notably, he
was the nephew of Lady Anne Hyde, wife of the man who
would become King James II, and a cousin to Queen Anne.
Educated at Oxford, he was a horseman in the king's royal
regiment, a member of Parliament and a dignitary in the court
of James, although he abandoned his sovereign in the Glorious
Revolution of 1688 in favor of William of Orange. Naturally
he was savaged for switching sides by the losers, who called
him a vainglorious drunk and a fool.

These were turbulent years, obviously, and part of the
backstory is the degree of vitriol that echoed through the hall-
ways and chambers among the nobles as various factions tried
to destroy their political enemies. Political operatives today
who have been brought up to think they know a thing or two
about mudslinging wouldn't have had a chance in those days
of vendetta, conspiracy, slander, and printed warfare.

Cornbury was, according to a Delaware County,
Pennsylvania, history, "a source of constant sorrow to his
father, (who was) a profligate, who had sounded every depth of
vice in Great Britain until he had become so involved in debt
by his excesses that his cousin, her gracious majesty, Queene
Anne, weary of his importunities and to remove him from her
presence, appointed him governor of the provinces of New
York and the Jerseys."

Escaping this messy cauldron of debt and intrigue—or at
least trading a fire in for a mere frying pan—Cornbury was
appointed to his new post by King William a year before his
cousin Anne's coronation. He might have been a fool, but he

had wisely chosen the winning side in the ongoing English drama, and was rewarded for it. His reward was also convenient in that it helped him escape a growing list of creditors who stalked him at every street corner.

He sailed to New York and took up residence in the fort at the southern tip of Manhattan known as the Bowling Green. He was unpopular almost from the beginning, although this would have been nothing remarkable. In the colonies, appointed governors and their elected assemblies were frequently at each others' throats, usually over salaries, land, or any other item of wealth or privilege. And it was clear that money and glory ranked high on Cornbury's list; he insisted, for example, on being called "His High Mightiness."

Indeed, Cornbury began to assert his will, dismissing public servants he didn't like, changing election law, and confiscating property. When yellow fever struck New York City, he fled to the community of Jamaica on Long Island, where for his temporary home he seized a Presbyterian parsonage on the grounds the minister was preaching without a license. He then kicked the congregation out of its own church, and when the Presbyterians retaliated by destroying the inner furnishings of the church, Cornbury trumped up charges on which they were fined or imprisoned.

And on it goes. Through the years Cornbury has been accused of malfeasance both public (keeping money that was to be used for the colony's defense for himself) and private (failing to give his wife a clothing budget).

But it was the manner of dress that attracted the most attention. In 1702, he was said to have presided over the Assembly in a formal, female robe that, in his defense, he said was meant to honor his cousin Anne. "You are very stupid not to see the propriety of it," he told an audience of presumably stupefied politicians. "In this place and particularly on this occasion I represent a woman and ought in all respects to represent her as faithfully as I can." This wouldn't have been the only way the frequently pickled governor was faithfully representing his cousin, whose florid nose and cheeks had earned her the title of Brandy Nan.

As time went on and Cornbury became more despised, stories began to spread about the governor's increasingly frequent cross-dressing. He did business with street merchants while he wore female attire and was also rumored to have shown up at his wife's 1706 funeral in a gown. Cross-dressing wasn't unknown in those days—a French spy at the time of the American Revolution spent decades masquerading as a woman, and so confused the curious public that a male/female-betting line generated lively interest on the London Stock Exchange. Frequently there was an objective (women wanting to serve in the military or men infiltrating a rival court) but not always. So the Cornbury stories were entirely plausible.

The problem in all this, as pointed out by historian Patricia Bonomi, who researched the rumors extensively, is that the sources of the cross-dressing stories originated from his political enemies, who in that particular age were, as established, not prone to be charitable. Colonist Lewis Morris wrote of Cornbury's "dressing publicly in woman's clothes every day, and putting a stop to all public business while he is pleasing himself with that peculiar but detestable (habit)." But Lewis was a staunch enemy, which calls this snippet of gossip into question. As was William Penn— whose Quakers had been treated shamefully by Cornbury—who, after a meeting with the governor in Philadelphia in 1703, called Cornbury "a man of luxury and poverty." The inference was clear, but so was the fact that Penn had an ax to grind. Penn said Cornbury was "possessed of many vices and few virtues" but, sadly, was no more specific than that.

Other sources of cross-dressing references were either second hand or bandied about long after Cornbury's death. In a paper prepared for the Delaware County, Pa., Historical Society, H. G. Ashmead called Cornbury "as abandoned a scoundrel as ever distressed those to whom he was kin by his ill deeds or cursed a people by his misrule." But Ashmead was writing about the governor two centuries after his time.

Ashmead culled his information from a visit Cornbury paid to the area, which by the sounds of it was anticipated by the locals much as they might have looked forward to a circus freak show. But in this regard, the governor's visit to Chester County, Pennsylvania, was a disappointment. Cornbury's only fashion *faux pas*, if the stories handed down through the years are accurate, was a pair of leather stockings, which generated considerable comment. That the populace at the time was on such high alert in regard to the governor's dress might lend a fillip of legitimacy to any cross-dressing proclivities.

Indeed, Ashmead believed that "When his lordship was beastly drunk . . . a common pasttime of his lordship—forgetful of his age and the office he held—was to attire himself in quilted petticoats, panier hoops and other accessories of dress then worn by women of fashion."

Walking alone at dusk, the governor opened himself up to all manner of groping from the night watchmen, which might or might not be welcome, but almost always left the sentries clutching at their hearts when they discovered whom they were attempting to diddle.

It's unclear whether, if the cross-dressing stories are true, there were a sexual element to Cornbury's behavior. There are no specific references in print beyond allegations of perversion and debauchery, which of course could be referring to dress alone. But this was not an open topic of discussion in those times (even in politics) and ideas of transvestites, transgenders, and the whole Rocky Horror Picture Show phenomenon would have drawn blank stares from the main of the eighteenth- century populace.

Although this cross-dressing governor is taken as an article of faith by many, if not most, historians, Patricia Bonomi doesn't buy it. "Of what evidence for Cornbury's presumed derelictions consist?" she wrote. "Surprisingly little, once it is sifted and isolated for scrutiny. Three colonials, all members of an opposition faction that rose against Governor Cornbury's imperial program in New York and New Jersey, wrote four letters between 1707 and 1709 relaying a rumor that Governor Cornbury frequently wore women's clothes. In addition, a few early documents include vague and contradictory charges that he took bribes and misappropriated government funds. There the contemporary trail of evidence falls off."

Considering that early eighteenth-century politicians would say most anything to smear their adversaries, this evidence is hardly credible, she said.

Further, a search of British records turns up no references that would back up Cornbury's enemies, she says. In an era when gossip was like oxygen, it's hard to think that stories of Cornbury's extravagances and crimes wouldn't have made it back home.

What did make it back home was Cornbury himself, called back by the queen herself who was tired of enduring ribbing she was taking for her relative's proclivities. Cornbury, by this time, was in debtor's prison, his lavish lifestyle having finally, once and for all, raced past his paucity of income.

Bonomi writes that "Considerable evidence suggests that the royal governors often responsibly administered their colonies to serve what they reasonably believed was the greater good of their empires." This might be true. And it is also true that American revolutionaries who wrote the history of the young country were not inclined to be charitable to former agents of the British crown. But there are several problems that follow from giving these British governors the benefit of the doubt. One, they usually did have to come to America after having worn out their welcome in their mother country. Second, the record shows that they were unable to deal with day-to-day problems that arose in their territories. And finally, had the governors administered wisely and even-handedly, the Revolution might never have happened.

All this, of course, is not enough to convict poor Cornbury beyond a reasonable doubt. But it is also worth noting that he had plenty of shortcomings that his enemies could have conveniently exploited without needing to make up a story about his clothing preferences out of, as it were, whole cloth. Nor was cross-dressing a go-to accusation for colonists seeking to discredit their gubernatorial enemies. The evidence might indeed be slim, but it is still evidence.

The one last loose end to tie up hangs in the New York Historical Society, and has been generally accepted to be a portrait of Cornbury in women's clothes. The portrait is indeed either that of a rather effeminate man, or of a woman who does not share the typical feminine traits. It's difficult to say which—the subject's rouge seems to be battling a five o'clock shadow for supremacy. The hands are delicate, but the jaw isn't.

The work is depicted as "Portrait of an Unidentified Woman," by the gallery, and its label goes on to say, "Typical of provincial British portraiture of the early eighteenth century, this rather curious portrait of a woman had long been identified as a likeness of Edward Hyde, who carried the title Viscount Cornbury and was appointed Governor of the Province of New York and New Jersey by his cousin, Queen Anne, in 1702. Serving as governor until 1708, Lord Cornbury was reported to have been 'universally detested,' and a fondness for cross-dressing accompanied his reputation as 'half-witted.'"

The label goes on to absolve Cornbury of some of these slanders, but notes that the unknown artist did, for whatever reason, refrain from making the woman, if a woman she be, seem more ladylike.

Bonomi doubted that it was Cornbury at all, while Dr. Philip Davenport-Hines, a fellow of the Royal Historical Society maintained that it was indeed the rogue governor in question, noting the subject's impish smirk. The does-he or doesn't-he question, barring some undiscovered cache of evidence, is unlikely to be settled. Dr. Marc Mappen, a Rutgers University dean quoted in the *New York Times* in 1990 prudently observed: "It's wonderful that an accepted interpretation is being challenged by new evidence. One of the great things about the study of history is that it's not written in stone."

Chapter 9

A Deadly Battle of Shakespearean Actors

Born in Philadelphia in 1806, Edwin Forrest was one of America's first home-grown global superstars. A Shakespearean actor, he amassed fame and fortune that today might be associated with the likes of George Clooney or Tiger Woods. Without all the electronic diversions of today, live theater in the nineteenth century equated not only to modern cinema, but to sporting events, rock concerts, and video games. Even countrified ruffians from unheard of backwaters could walk around quoting Shakespeare, just as twenty-first-century geeks parrot Monty Python.

Theater was also relatively new as an accepted form of entertainment, at least in the Northeast, where those colonies that hadn't already banned stage productions were urged to do so by no less an authority than the Continental Congress. If that wasn't good enough, there were holier opponents. "The man who sees the final issue of the matter, must be mad indeed, if for the momentary carnal enjoyment of a visionary illusion, he consent to lose his soul," thundered Timothy Dwight IV, president of Yale at the turn of the nineteenth century. Calling theater "naked and filthy," he seemed appalled that there could even be another side to the issue.

As the theaters began to proliferate (occasionally under the ruse of calling themselves a "Music Academy" or some such), they also took on a political air. There were theaters for the masses and theaters for the aristocrats, and correspondingly there were actors who inspired those in either high or low places.

Edwin Forrest was a hero to Americans and he was a hero to working class Americans all the more. He was, according to an account by contemporary H. M. Ranney, "born into a humble life and worked his way from poverty and obscurity to wealth and fame, by the power of genius." And his style was quintessentially American. When playing a Shakespearean character on stage he would jettison the boring lines and focus on action. It was, says University of Maryland Associate Professor Heather S. Nathans, "action packed, moving along like a summer blockbuster from explosion to explosion."

By contrast, the English actor William Macready—a chief rival of Forrest's, in Forrest's eyes, at least—was intellectual and detail oriented, his disposition more in tune with gentler, introspective roles. Even so, he was well received in tours of the United States, a circumstance that may have somewhat provoked Forrest, despite the American's assertion that the two were on generally good terms.

If that were the case, it ended on a night in Edinburgh in the spring of 1846, where Macready was on stage and Forrest was in the audience. Macready was performing *Hamlet* and at some point decided the sad prince might benefit from a little song and dance number. There wasn't anything terribly odd about this—critics today who shudder it the idea of changing a single word of the bard's work would faint dead away at early-1800s productions where ad lib was the rule.

Even so, Forrest thought this was a pirouette too far, and let loose with the hiss heard 'round the world. Before all was said and done, twenty-five people would be killed on the streets of New York as the result of this imprudent outburst.

British sensibilities were badly damaged by this boorish behavior, especially considering the source. It would have been one thing for an average theater-goer to voice displeasure with the stunt, but for a rival actor—when touring, the two performers often went head-to-head at competing theaters—it was considered to be exceedingly bad manners. Forrest was roundly criticized and his audiences waned to the point that he felt the need to defend himself in a letter to the editor of the *London Times*. Forrest said the hiss was nothing more than a little constructive criticism, contended others hissed as well, said that hissing was a natural part of theater and finally, a dance? In *Hamlet*? Are you *serious*?

But Forrest was on unfriendly soil, and this was a battle he would not win. At least not across the Atlantic. But as word of the kerfuffle made its way back to the states, sentiments ran strongly away from Macready and in favor of Forrest. American partisans recalled the time back in 1827 when Macready, playing William Tell in Baltimore, had pitched a fit because the stage manager had failed to provide him with suitable arrows. Macready asked what was so bloody hard about "get[ing] such an arrow in your country, sir!" Among the rowdier factions of theater fans, this translated into an insult against the United States of America.

When Macready made his return to America in October, 1848, the country was loaded for bear. Not only was he a foreigner, he represented the upper class, an "actor-autocrat" who, wrote the *Boston Mail*, "refuses to show himself for less than a dollar a ticket."

"[W]e only pity his ignorance of the institutions of this country," the editor continued, "and hope for his own credit's sake that that he will not, when he gets home, write a black book about American manners . . . but if he does that he will spare us in the production of his brain."

At this point the *Mail* was just getting warmed up, but the central accusation was that Macready had secretly torpedoed Forrest's most recent tour of England out of professional jealousy. Both Macready and Forrest were playing in Boston at the time, and the setting seemed ripe for a confrontation. "But the Bostonians are a quiet people," wrote Ranney, "and Macready and Forrest played through their engagements without any popular demonstrations."

But that was Boston. The next stop on the tour was New York.

By this time, Shakespeare was becoming a secondary form of entertainment. The actors were using the stage and newspaper columns to air their gripes about each other in public, Macready not even willing to call Forrest by name, referring to him only as "an American actor." Forrest referred to Macready as "that poor old man" or, better, a "superannuated driveler."

Macready swore that the two had been quite cordial prior to the hissing in question, an assertion that was too much for Forrest. "Bah!" he wrote in the papers. "Mr. Macready has no feeling of kindness for any actor who is likely, by his talent, to stand in his way."

Forrest reported that, while in England, Macready's cronies had dogged him at every performance, trying to hiss him off the stage, and went on in a fiery screed to call names and hurl accusations at his rival. This mudslinging generally horrified the American aristocracy, but it was bloody chum for the dirty-faced teenage boys who ran the cities' printing presses, mended their wagons and butchered their cattle. All were patrons of the theater, just as today the Cineplex attracts a cross section of society. The difference was that the rich sat in private boxes, while the apprentices sat in the balconies, which, conveniently enough, provided satisfactory trajectories for the spoiled fruit and vegetables they routinely brought to the show should some aspect of the performance dissatisfy them.

In the growing dispute, the boys of New York were inspired by patriotism as well as class. The War of 1812 wasn't that far in the rear view mirror, and just a decade prior a bloodless confrontation known as the Aroostook War pitted Britain against America in a dispute over the Maine border. So by the time Macready had arrived on American shores, Ranney wrote, "the flame of hatred was ready to burst forth, and the only wonder is that it remained pent up so long."

On Monday, May 7, Macready was booked to perform *Macbeth* at the Astor Opera House, a grand Parthenon of a building on Lafayette Street between Astor Place and East Eighth Street. The venue was not helpful. Less than two years old, the Opera House had specifically been designed, wrote author and editor Nathaniel Parker Willis, as "a refined attraction which the ill-mannered would not be likely to frequent, and around which the higher classes might gather" without fear of random rotten-tomato spatter. Unfortunately for all concerned, there were still five hundred seats for the great unwashed in the upper balconies, segregated from the upper crust, but still within range for catcalls and unsavory missiles.

Forrest was playing simultaneously at the nearby Broadway Theater, but it was Macready that Forrest's fans were clamoring to see. When the Englishman stepped onto the stage, the upper reaches of the theater erupted in a cacophony of hisses, jeers, and groan. The great actor was not intimidated, however, and the show went on, even if no one could hear his lines. Neither did the peanut gallery pipe down, and when word leaked out that they possessed packets of gunpowder that they planned to throw into the gas chandelier, the owners stepped in and drew the curtain.

A rational person might have assumed that this was the end of Macready's run in New York—Macready himself certainly thought so. But then Washington Irving got involved. The great American author led a contingent of New York luminaries who implored Macready not to give in to the rabble, and with the encouragement of Forrest's detractors, he agreed to another performance on May 10.

This was further incitement to the city's working class, which had assumed along with most everyone else that it had driven a stake through Macready's stage career in the city. Now, along with the British, these young toughs had another enemy in their sights—the privileged elite who had banished them to the balconies. Wrote Ranney, "Macready was a subordinate personage, and he was to be put down less on his own account, than to spite his aristocratic supporters. It was rich against the poor—the aristocracy against the people. The rich and well-bred are too apt to despise the poor and ignorant, and they must not think it strange when they are hated in return."

If the seventh had been bad, the tenth was bound to be worse, and the city fathers begged the owners of the Astor to reconsider. But controversy was good for business, and citing their rights to do business, the owners declared that she show would go on.

As handbills went up and Forrest partisans scarfed up tickets, New York's Mayor Woodhull again appealed to the owners to call off the show and avert what was brewing as a near-certain riot. Again rebuffed, the mayor called in his chief of police and, more ominously, several companies of US soldiers. The rumor of a riot and the fact of military involvement combined to draw thousands of people to Astor Place who wouldn't have been there otherwise. Contemporaries reckoned it had been a decade since the city's last decent riot (unlike in nineteenth-century Philadelphia, where even before the advent of professional football, civic disturbances were by the sounds of it a biweekly occurrence) and no one wanted to miss the fun.

In accordance with the owners' hopes, the theater sold out quickly that evening, and hundreds, then thousands of bystanders milled around the plaza in anticipation of the end-game. Inside, Macready was roundly cheered by the elites and roundly jeered by the rabble in an unending eruption of noise that of course totally disrupted the show. At one point a hastily drawn sign appeared on stage, advising "The Friends of

Order Will Remain Quiet." But as Ranney dryly noted, it was the friends of disorder who had the more leathery lungs. The police finally began to get the upper hand inside, but outside things were rapidly deteriorating. A nearby public sewer project provided stacks of paving stones that the crowd—by this time estimated at upwards of ten thousand to fifteen thousand strong—appropriated for the purpose of smashing windows, doors, and the occasional unlucky officer of the law. Macready got away by disguising himself as a cop, and it is only a slight exaggeration to say that, scared for life and limb, he was halfway across the Atlantic by evening's end.

What remained behind was a scene of complete chaos. The police were no match for the mob, and New York's finest were more than happy to turn the job over to Major General Charles Sandford and the military, which waded into the fray, bayonets at the ready. The sight of US soldiers bearing arms against their fellow countrymen did not have the calming effect New York authorities had hoped. Just the opposite. The mob surged toward a line of horsemen riding from Broadway to Astor Place, spooking animals unaccustomed to riots. Their riders went flying into the crowd, and a following bayonet charge failed because the soldiers were unable to level their weapons in the dense mass of humanity.

Then, whether out of frustration, panic or fear, the unthinkable happened. The order came down the line to open fire.

A sheet of flame and rattle of rifles erupted in the night and here and there a man fell. Officers later testified they had ordered their men to fire over the heads of rioters, but in the melee, not everyone got the message. As the soldiers tried to push the crowd back toward the Bowery, the deadliness of the gunfire was not readily apparent. Some assumed the soldiers were firing over the heads of the people, and some were. But others weren't. It was initially assumed that those who fell were themselves play-acting, and only when blood began pooling around their bodies did the truth become apparent. Instead of running, the mob reacted with fury. Its thrust was finally beaten back with repeated volleys of gunfire. It took longer than it should for the seriousness of the situation to set in, but when it did, rioters and sightseers scattered in all directions. As smoke mixed with the night mist, an awful, stunned quiet fell upon the scene, broken only by the groans and cries of the wounded. Twenty-two people lay dead or mortally wounded. Another thirty or so were wounded, some maimed for life.

Many of those who paid the most dearly were not rioters at all, but spectators, or those simply trying to make their way through town. Bridget Fagan was walking along the Bowery with her husband when a stray shot struck her leg, a wound from which she did not survive. Likewise was a man shot dead as he was getting off a car of the Harlem Railroad. A bullet pierced the brain of Wall Street broker George Gedney as he stood outside the Langdon mansion, where he'd posted himself to watch; he'd been married a year and had a newborn child.

The disturbance lasted well into the next day. A hastily formed committee by the likely enough name "Citizens Opposed to the Destruction of Human Life" called for the indictment of the mayor, recorder, and sheriff. Several thousand people attended the rally, passing resolutions that insisted the authorities had per-petuated "the most wanton, unprovoked and murderous outrage ever perpetuated in the civilized world." That night rumors flew that the opera house would be burned to the ground, but this time Sandford made an emphatic show of force: one troop of horse artillery, one squadron of cavalry, four regiments of infantry, and for good measure a twenty-four-pound Howitzer.

Again a mob pushed up Broadway, but this time—having learned from experience—the reaction on the part of authorities was more efficient and restrained. Key leaders of the riot were arrested and the crowd was given ample warning that violence would meet with deadly force. Order was restored to the city, despite rumors that the people of Philadelphia had heard that good rioting was to be had in New York and were venturing to the city to take part.

A jury was called to examine the shootings, and concluded that authorities had no choice but to fire. It added, however, that the shooting might not have been necessary had the police, who had plenty of advance notice that a disturbance was in the works, had been proactive.

In the end, calmer heads concluded that Macready's second performance should never have been allowed to happen. With an eye only on a packed house and resulting profits, the theater owners convinced the city fathers to allow the show to go on. Macready deeply regretted his second show at the opera house. Some blamed Forrest, contending that the American actor had secretly agitated among his partisans for the riot—a claim he successfully quelled by threatening libel suits. But the truth was, no one performed well that night and twenty-five people paid with their lives. Nor did the Astor Place Theater survive. It became known as the Massacre Opera House at (Dis)Astor Place, a reputation not conducive to ticket sales. It was gutted in 1853, and sold to the New York Mercantile Library, which renamed the building Clinton Hall. In 1890 the theater was torn down.

CHAPTER 10

Woodlawn Cemetery's Celebrated Clientele

L ife and death have seldom danced cheek to cheek with such elegance as they have for better than 150 years at the Woodlawn cemetery in the Bronx. At Woodlawn, flowers bloom, brooks babble, and the works of man at his artistic and masonic best sprout from the green earth—works and words inspired by those who now rest below. Woodlawn opened in 1863 when people were dying right and left in the Civil War, but, unlike many famous burial grounds, the cemetery is known less for war dead than for cultural and industrial luminaries whose lives befit a special piece of the ground on which they used to walk.

When Herman Melville went to that great shipyard in the sky, Woodlawn became his final place of rest, keeping company with artists of all sorts. What music might be made by the cemetery's house band, which would include Irving Berlin, Miles Davis, and Duke Ellington? At Woodlawn the beauty of art meets the beasts of finance and industry. What devious deals could be cut by Jay Gould and Collis Huntington? And leave the housewares to Rowland Macy and J. C. Penney. Let Joseph Pulitzer tell the story.

And what a story. The population, as such, of three hundred thousand, would dwarf that of the largest cities in a handful of rural states such as Montana, Wyoming, and West Virginia. The four hundred-acre cemetery is about half the size of Central Park—and in keeping with Central Park, the sons of its designer, Frederick Law Olmsted are buried in Woodlawn. It's fitting then that Woodlawn is an architectural and landscaping candy store. Its monuments and mausoleums were designed by a who's who of American architects and designers (some buried there, some not), from John Russell Pope, architect of the National Gallery of Art and the Jefferson Memorial, to Stanford White, the consensus artist-in-residence of the Gilded Age.

But giving monuments and landscaping their due, the people make the cemetery, and along with the shining stars, there are countless lesser known individuals whose stories are every bit as compelling and worth the retelling.

Take for example, Tex Rickard, who was born in 1870 and became known at the P. T. Barnum of sports. Think of him as Don King without the hair. Born in Kansas City, he briefly served as a marshal in Henrietta, Texas, before becoming swept up in the Alaskan Gold Rush. Arriving in the Klondike in 1897, Rickard staked some lucrative claims that he and a partner sold for a staggering sum of $60,000. He then (cliché as it might be) gambled away the cash and lost the saloon that he had had bought with the loot. There was little to do but pull up stakes and move on to Nome, where the next rush was in high gear, and do it all over again.

Which he might have done, had he not run into, of all people, the great Wild West lawman, Wyatt Earp. The two became fast friends, interested as they both were in running bars and promoting prize fights. By the 1920s, Rickard was back in the States, where he wrangled the rights to promote live events at Madison Square Garden. There he brought the sport of boxing into the public eye, largely on the broad shoulders of his most famous client, Jack Dempsy.

Needing a bigger and better venue for his events, the former prospector lined up financing for the third incarnation of the great New York icon Madison Square Garden, a property that had by that time achieved a lengthy history of, in no particular order, sports, munitions, and bad boys. A US arsenal dominated the property in the early 1800s, and from there it transitioned into the New York House of Refuge for the Society of the Protection of Juvenile Delinquents. The reform house burned in 1839, and a roadhouse took its place for travelers to and from the city. The proprietors named it Madison Cottage, after the recent president, and the name stuck through the years, giving birth to Madison Avenue and Madison Square Park.

The first Madison Square Garden, built in 1879, was leased to P. T. Barnum; it failed, primarily because it lacked a roof. The second, more elegant Madison Square Garden was designed by Stanford White and built in 1890. For a time its thirty-two-story bell tower made it the city's second-tallest building.

Madison Square Garden III was known as the House That Tex Built and the hockey team he assembled to play there became playfully named "Tex's Rangers." These New York Rangers won the Stanley Cup in 1928, their second year, and the blueshirts have been beloved ever since. Fans come each spring to place trinkets at Rickards' Woodlawn headstone which, considering his showman's flair, is rather conservative in its design. Paying homage to Rickard's stone, it is hoped, will bring the Rangers good luck in the upcoming season.

Isidor Straus, another Woodlawn resident, could have used a little luck in the spring of 1912 as he and his wife Ida were vacationing in the south of France. Life had been good to the German-born Straus, who had come to America in 1854 as a boy and with his father and brother sold dishes in the basement of a dry goods store owned by Rowland Macy. In the beginning, Macy didn't make an overpowering success of things, trying and failing four times to get a business up and running. Success came in 1858, when Macy bet on northward expansion of the city, and located a store at Sixth Avenue between 13th and 14th streets. R. H. Macy & Co.—its trademark red star taken from a tattoo Macy received while serving on a whaling ship as a teen—took in the equivalent of $300 on its first day and never looked back. But Macy wouldn't live to see the store's greatest days. He died young, at age fifty-four, of kidney failure and was interred at Woodlawn in 1877. By the end of the century, Straus and his brother had taken full ownership of Macy's department store and, taking a page out of Macy's original playbook, moved Macy's flagship store uptown to Herald Square at 34th and Broadway. Until development caught up, Straus ferried customers from Lower Manhattan to his new store in a steam-powered bus.

Having been blessed with much, Straus returned much in the areas of philanthropy and public service. He served briefly in Congress, was an ambassador to France, and was a champion of education and public-employee reforms. President Grover Cleveland offered him the job of postmaster general, which he declined. But his celebrity, as such, wasn't sealed until, returning to the United States from France, he and his wife booked a stateroom on the *RMS Titanic*.

Neither would survive the journey. But the couple's love, heroism, and devotion to each other in their last hours made them legend. As the doomed ship was sinking into the icy North Atlantic, the crew attempted to usher Ida into a waiting lifeboat. She refused, however, to abandon her husband. Quickly assessing the situation, an officer reckoned there would be room for Isidor in the same lifeboat, but survivors reported that Straus refused to go before other men, and while women and children were still on board. That settled it. Ida saw to it that her maid was seated in a lifeboat, and as they parted, handed her fur coat to the woman, saying she would have no future need of it. Survivors of the wreck reported catching a final glimpse of the couple, as they stood calmly on the deck watching events take their course.

Isidor's body was recovered, Ida's wasn't. But they are commemorated together at the Straus mausoleum at Woodlawn with a quote from the Song of Solomon: "Many waters cannot quench love—neither can the floods drown it."

A happier occasion on the high seas of the Atlantic—and one more story that would end at Woodlawn—had occurred in 1836 as a Protestant couple from Burgundy in France was sailing to America. Jean Nicholas Juilliard was a shoemaker who, in the midst of America's great cotton boom, correctly sensed opportunities in textiles in the States. In middle of the Atlantic, his wife Anna gave birth to a son, Augustus Juilliard, and the young family went on to settle in Ohio. From the time he first made a little change working in a dry goods store, Augustus had a head for business. He was also blessed with other advantages, becoming friends with a young William McKinley, destined to become president, and strong communication skills heightened in international circles by his fluency in French. His obituary noted that "Juilliard was an informed and vigorous protectionist [considered to be a good thing at the time], and the strength and wisdom of his economic views and the vigor with which they were expressed had made a profound impression upon his fellow business men and upon the country."

Juilliard moved to New York and made a name for himself trading textiles futures contracts. When the Panic of 1873 drove the esteemed Hoyt, Sprague & Co.—the city's largest trading shop—into bankruptcy, Juilliard was named receiver. Out of the ruins, he built the A. D. Juilliard & Co. empire, which manufactured and made markets in textiles, taking great advantage of the vast sheets of fabric needed for the sails of the world's great ships.

Juilliard's dossier would have done any captain of industry in the industrial revolution proud: He was a director of the National Bank of Commerce; the Bank of America; the Atchison, Topeka, and Santa Fe Railroad; New York Life Insurance and Trust Co.; the Mutual Life Insurance Co.; and various other trust and real estate companies. He is, after a fashion, the reason that the paper money in America gained legal acceptance. In 1879, a Connecticut trader named Thomas Greenman purchased one hundred bales of cotton from Juilliard for $5,122.90 and paid for it, or attempted to anyway, with $22.90 in gold and silver and $5,100 in paper notes.

On the heels of the1873 Panic, a financial catastrophe that wouldn't be one-upped until the 1930s, this was a touchy subject. Congress and the courts had gone back and forth over the legality of paper money, and Juilliard for one was convinced that only silver and gold could legally satisfy a debt. Paper money, or greenbacks, were a product of the Civil War, at a time when meeting payroll for hundreds of thousands of men and paying for freight trains worth of hay with sacks of silver and gold were obviously problematic. While it was acknowledged that paper money was acceptable in a wartime emergency, those of Juilliard's mind felt that in quieter times there was no obligation to accept these notes for payment. Juilliard pursued this notion all the way to the Supreme Court—and quite obviously lost.

But as accomplished as he was in life, it was his death that rocked the city. His business dealings had been half the story, the other half being a strong presence in the arts. He was active in the Metropolitan Opera, the Metropolitan Museum, of Art, and the American Museum of Natural History. And when his will was read in 1919, the *New York Times* reported that "After providing for the immediate relatives and making bequests of $100,000 each to various institutions, the will sets aside the entire residuary estate, conservatively estimated to be considerably more than $5,000,000 for the establishment of the Juilliard Musical Foundation."

Save for one or maybe two family members, no one had any inkling that the gift, which worked out to be nearly three times what was originally reported, was in the works. Juilliard, the school, if not the man, became legend. By the Juilliard School's count, its alumni have won more than 105 Grammy Awards, 62 Tony Awards, 47 Emmy Awards, 26 Bessie Awards, 24 Academy Awards, 16 Pulitzer Prizes, and 12 National Medals for the Arts. Juilliard the man rests in a handsome mausoleum at Woodlawn, comforted, perhaps by the surplus of musicians who share the same grounds.

Yet in deference to Juilliard and the other captains of industry who built financial fortunes and empires, the most astonishing financial success story of all those who rest in Woodlawn might not go to a white baron, but a black baroness, the remarkable Madam C. J. Walker.

Born in a small, Louisiana town in 1867 as Sarah Breedlove, Walker escaped being born a slave by only five years. Her parents and older siblings were enslaved on a Madison Parish plantation that would become a logistical staging area for Gen. Ulysses Grant's attack on Vicksburg in 1863, which proved so pivotal in turning the tide of the Civil War.

But free didn't translate into easy. Walker's parents died young, leaving her with a sister and abusive brother-in-law. She married at age 14, if for no other reason than to get out of the house, and her own husband died six years later, leaving her with a two-year-old daughter and little prospect of amounting to anything memorable, as far as the world was concerned. She settled in St. Louis in the care of her brothers, where she became a washerwoman on what today would be an annual wage of about $6,500.

But Walker was blessed—she wouldn't have used that word at the time—with chronic scalp ailments and hair loss brought about by shampooing with lye. In rural America at this point and time, bathing and the washing of hair might be a monthly occurrence. And the thought of caring and even styling one's hair was as alien as silver soup terrines. Definitely, there was an open market to be had. It was her brothers, three of them barbers, who taught her proper hair care and planted the seed for Walker's empire. The responsibility for nurturing this seed fell to another female African American entrepreneur named Annie Malone, the daughter of an escaped slave who parlayed an interest in hairdressing and a love of chemistry into a multimillion-dollar fortune in cosmetics.

Lye wasn't the only enemy of hair at the turn of the twentieth century. Black women straightened their curls with what must have been a fragrant assortment of animal oils, bacon fat, and goose grease, none of which was follicle-affirming. Malone's Wonderful Hair Grower straightened hair without the damage. But her genius wasn't just in product, it was in the way she marketed and sold it. Malone took advantage of mass media, press conferences, and freebies to generate demand, which was met by door-to-door sales women. (Annie Malone survived in spite of men rather than because of them; she quickly divorced one meddling husband, but was not so lucky with her second, who hung on long enough for half of her fortune in divorce proceedings.)

Above all, perhaps, Malone took pride in teaching young women to succeed—how to dress, speak, and act in the business world. She created a manufacturing plant and college that is credited with creating seventy-five thousand jobs internationally. One of her protégés was Walker, who patterned her business model after Malone's. She added a mail order component and eventually sold hair-care products and cosmetics throughout the Southeast, the Caribbean, and Central America. Madam C. J. Malone (the name was drawn from her second husband, a newspaper ad man, Charles Joseph Walker) greatly impacted black business and black women. Still, she has viewed with some suspicion both by her contemporaries and by history. Some black stalwarts at the time kept their distance, unconvinced that hair products were the proper foundation upon which to base racial equality. By the 1960s, forty years after Walker's death, hair had become politicized. Long hair, of course, was symbolic of peaceniks, while afros became a symbol of black power. The notion of straightening black hair was akin to selling out to the white race. But Malone promoted healthy hair, not straight hair, wrote her great-great-granddaughter A'Lelia Bundles in the book *On Her Own Ground: The Life and Times of Madam C. J. Walker*, and bristled when a white newspaper called her "the de-kink queen." "I deplore such an impression," Bundles quotes Walker telling a reporter in 1918, "because I have always held myself out as a hair culturist. I grow hair." Newspaper notices referred to her as a culturist as well, and wrote of her demonstrations on "the art of growing hair."

She was equally adept at the art of growing her business, not an easy task for a black woman lacking a formal education in a white business world where almost every conceivable card was stacked against her. This was still a world where a woman, no matter how successful, was still not allowed to vote. Failing to attract black investors (including the much-courted Booker T. Washington) and understandably dubious of white capitalists who would be all too happy to invest—and take control—of her company, Walker scraped to come up with the money for the Madam C. J. Walker Manufacturing Company of Indiana, a complex that included a research lab and a school which taught women how to sell products and how to survive in the business world.

By the time she moved to New York shortly before her death, she had naturally drifted into the world of philan-thropy and politics, putting up donations for black social and recreational facilities and antilynching funds and agitat-ing for racial equality. Walker joined the New York chapter of the fledgling NAACP, which organized the Silent Parade, a gathering of ten thousand marching down Fifth Avenue in protest of the dozens who were killed in 1917 race riots in East St. Louis.

She also led a fight for justice for black soldiers of World War I, which was an epic time in the advancement of African Americans' station in life. The War came on the cusp of the Great Migration, when conscription in Europe deprived New York and the other great northern cities of dependable supplies of cheap immigrant labor.

Southern whites devoid of any sense of irony, howled in protest when blacks picked up and headed to the cities, a demo-graphic shift the led southerners to accuse the North of unfair labor practices, which basically amounted to giving blacks a job (and, not coincidentally, the economic power to make a woman like Walker into a success). When the war arrived, it was generally greeted with disinterest by African American communities until President Woodrow Wilson's idea that the world must be made safe for democracy. This resonated. If the world playing field were to leveled, certainly too would America's. Democracy was the antidote to white supremacy.

There were warning signs, of course, that this would not be the case. A name on a government form was not helpful determining if the applicant were qualified for the task at hand, "qualified" being understood at the time as "white," so the Wilson administration required photos on Civil Service applications. Conscription offices took to tearing off the corner of draft cards submitted by African Americans, just so there wouldn't be any embarrassing misunderstanding on down the road. Still, blacks across America went out of their way to pledge loyalty. "If America truly understands the functions of democracy and justice, she must know that she must begin to promote democracy and justice at home first of all," said Arthur G. Shaw in a New York speech. African Americans supported the war not just with words but with their service.

The results were discouraging. Expecting, if not a hero's welcome, at least grudging admiration, black veterans were sorely disappointed. Fearing blacks would now demand equal treatment domestically, racial riots and lynchings escalated. Walker led a delegation to Washington to meet with Woodrow Wilson, but at the last minute the president said he would not be available.

Walker continued her activism even as her partners feared it would damage her business. "You must always bear in mind that you have a large business," wrote her general manager

Freeman Ransom, "whereas the other (activists) have nothing. There are many ways in which your business can be hampered so as to practically put you out of business."

Of course a woman who slayed so many of life's dragons was unlikely to be impressed with such logic. As she once famously snapped at a naysayer, "I am a woman who came from the cotton fields of the South. From there I was promoted to the washtub. From there I was promoted to the cook kitchen. And from there I promoted myself into the business of manufacturing hair goods and preparations. . . . I have built my own factory on my own ground."

From a ramshackle slave quarters on the Mississippi, Walker had done well enough to commission the stunning mansion Villa Lewaro on the Hudson, twenty miles north of Manhattan. The mansion was the crown jewel in the portfolio of Vertner Tandy, New York's first registered black architect. It was here she died of kidney failure in 1919, leaving a legacy that paved the way for Oprah Winfrey, Xerox CEO Ursula Burns, and Sam's Club CEO Rosalind Brewer.

Walker rests in Woodlawn shoulder to shoulder with a female who's who of national leaders, artists, entrepreneurs, agitators, and stars. There is the prima ballerina Marie Bonfanti and the Queen of Salsa, Celia Cruz, along with the great suffragists Carrie Chapman Catt, Elizabeth Cady Stanton, and Mary Garrett Hay. There are stories of success, such as Ruth Rowland Nichols who bested Charles Lindberg's transcontinental air speed record in 1930, and Margaret Rudkin who founded Pepperidge Farms. Maria Kraus-Boelte developed the concept of kindergarten; Gertrude Ederle was the first woman to swim the English Channel.

Along with successes were tragedies. Olive Thomas created a sensation when she won a "Most Beautiful Girl in New York" contest. She was dead in 1920 at age twenty-two after mistakenly drinking a syphilis medicine that was meant to be applied topically. Two years older at the time of her death in 1923 and apparently headed to stardom after appearing opposite John Barrymore, was Martha Mansfield, who died from her wounds after the hoop skirt of her Civil War costume was set afire by a carelessly tossed match.

Then there was Ruth Snyder, a housewife from Queens in 1925 who became disillusioned with her husband when he named his boat after his late girlfriend. Snyder had him take out a life insurance policy and tried, unsuccessfully, to kill him seven times. Her husband, a slow learner, it seems, continued to hang around and, sure enough, the eighth time was the charm. The investigation did not prove Snyder to be a master criminal (one wag in the press tarred it as the "dumb belle" murder), but she might have survived it if the police hadn't found a letter signed with the initials J. G. These were actually the initials of Jessie Guishard, the aforementioned girlfriend of the departed husband—coincidentally, however, Snyder was seeing a man named Judd Gray, and she assumed that was who the police were talking about. When they asked her about J. G., Snyder asked what Judd Gray had to do with anything, and the police said "Who's Judd Gray?" Classic.

Poor Judd, who had played a reluctant role in the murder was hauled in for questioning and almost immediately confessed, although each blamed the other for being the mastermind. It didn't matter, both went to the chair. The crime is remembered not so much for the crime itself, but for newspaper photographer Tom Howard who surreptitiously strapped a camera to his leg and photographed Snyder as she was stepped to "Old Sparky in Sing Sing, with two thousand volts coursing through her body. The famous photograph created pandemonium when it ran the next day in the *Daily News*.

A happier life, presumably, was led by the "Queen of Happiness," Florence Mills, a popular entertainer in the twenties who died too young, at age thirty-two. Ten thousand came to her service, and a plane flew over her grave at Woodlawn dropping rose petals—another special day at New York's most special resting place.

CHAPTER 11

A Building and a Food Fight for the Ages

In popular circles, architect George B. Post is most noted as the designer of the iconic New York Stock Exchange building, with its democratically inspired neoclassical look and six mighty Corinthian columns soaring to a pediment fronted with a sculpture by John Quincy Adams Ward that rather opaquely depicts "Integrity Protecting the Works of Man." Aside from the fact that this ideal could only be applied very loosely to the world of finance, there were other, more structural problems. The ninety-ton marble sculpture proved too substantial for the pediment, and as alarming cracks began to show themselves, it was feared that the female figure representing Integrity might lose purchase and pancake an unwitting stockbroker on the street below. Thirty-two years after it went up, the sculpture was taken down and replaced with a (lighter) painted replica.

Post's best work, however, was an exchange that made a market not in securities, but in cotton oil, grain, hops, flour, and lard. The New York Produce Exchange was built in 1884 at 2 Broadway overlooking the Bowling Green. As long as a football field and capable of comfortably holding seven thousand men on its trading floor, the Produce Exchange with its russet brick and terra cotta facing remained an imposing structure, even as buildings around it were soaring to twice its height. The Produce Exchange was torn down in 1957 and replaced with a wince-worthy glass office building. "The Produce Exchange," wrote Nathan Silver in *Lost New York*, "one of the best buildings in New York, was replaced in 1957 by one of the worst." It was one of the city's greatest architectural tragedies.

The clientele of the two exchange buildings overlapped in 1903, when the Produce Exchange rented space to the NYSE as it was waiting for its new digs to open. The partnership was not particularly memorable except on the last day of the arrangement, at which point it became the scene of maybe the greatest food fight in the history of New York City. It was a moment of levity that was perhaps two centuries in the making.

The Produce Exchange was established in 1861, the first year of the American Civil War. But European trade at that point dated back to at least 1624 when the Dutch established a fur trading settlement in what would become Lower Manhattan. The city itself, of course, would become famous for trade, so perhaps it was fitting that the island itself changed hands several times after it was discovered by the Florentine explorer Giovanni de Verrazzano in 1524 and named New Angoulême in honor of the French king he was working for at the time. The southern tip of the island made for an obvious strategic stronghold, and within a year Fort Amsterdam was built, and with it was born the city of New Amsterdam which would be taken by the English and renamed New York in 1664. The Dutch recaptured the city and changed the name to New Orange not quite a decade later, but within a year they'd traded it back to the English for an island in Indonesia that grew nutmeg.

The Dutch established a marketplace in the shadow of their fort in 1658, which became known as the Broadway Shambles. The first building of commerce had an arched lower floor that left buyers and sellers open to the elements. The roof was of straw thatch. "Such a shelter the thrifty Hollander, even of that day, would have felt scarcely afforded adequate protection for his cattle," said the president of the Produce Exchange during the building's opening day ceremonies. "And yet . . . in that poor husk was stirring the germ of mercantile vitality which has grown to mighty proportions."

The old fort overlooked Bowling Green, a vast lawn that hosted daily farmers markets and frequent fairs. The fort was gone by 1790, replaced by a government office building, but trade in the general neighborhood was just getting started. At the site that would become the produce exchange, traders built storehouses that served the growing markets. One hundred years before the Revolution, a colonial governor wrote that trade included "provisions of all sorts, as of wheate exported yearly about 60,000 bushels, pease, beefe, pork and some fish, tobacco, etc."

A lot of this produce was grown farther and farther inland, and a better form of transport was necessary to get it to market. Most normal people, Thomas Jefferson among them, laughed to the point of tears at the idea of digging a ditch forty feet wide across the breadth of New York State, but not Gov. DeWitt Clinton, who convinced the legislature in 1817 to allocate $7 million for the Erie Canal. It was quite true that the cost and effort would be staggering. But even more staggering was the economic impact of connecting western farmlands with the Eastern Seaboard with a water route that reduced transportation costs by as much as 95 percent. It would be the only such water route through the imposing eastern mountains that, agriculturally speaking, separated producers from consumers. The railroads would not be long in coming, but for a couple of decades New York City, connected to the Great Lakes by the Erie Canal and Hudson River, enjoyed a tremendous trade advantage. One Exchange publication noted that "Soon after the canal was completed there began a great demand for American foodstuffs which resulted in the development of extensive milling interests, the building up of a fast clipper service between New York and Europe and all the wonders that accompanied the growth and development of American agriculture." Some even feared that the advantage was too good—that the city would become a mere turnstile for crops, raw materials, and finished products destined for more vibrant locales. Of course those fears were overblown, and in point of fact it was the canal that gave New York a permanent leg up over the other great Eastern port cities of Boston, Philadelphia, and Baltimore. And beyond that, New York's exploding population was becoming a market in itself. In 1840, dockworkers packed a remarkable ten thousand barrels of flour into a ship bound for Liverpool. For traders, this event was like the moon landing, and proof positive of the young nation's agriculture prowess. But in another seventy years, New Yorkers alone were consuming ten thousand barrels of flour in one day.

Writing in 1911, Produce Exchange President E. R. Carhart noted, "From the day when trade was an ever-unfolding romance down to the present when trade has become a fixed science, New York has been a gateway of American commerce. Her natural advantages gave her easy ascendancy over all her competitors." A half-century after the opening of the canal, there was "a period of intense activity, of almost superhuman endeavor, of colossal enterprise. . . ." Produce exchanges helped organize that energy. They did not set prices themselves, but traded information that allowed buyers and sellers to make educated decisions about the market value of the product at hand. At the exchange, the opinions of hundreds of traders were averaged out, much in the way a modern share price is reflective of thousands of ideas about what a stock is worth.

Various exchange buildings dated back to 1690 at the southern end of Broad Street, and the first true grain exchange—little more than a shed known as the Meal Market—was slapped together at the lower end of Wall Street in the 1720s. By law, it was the only place in the city allowed to wholesale corn, grain, and meal. After the Revolution, of course, anything with the word "royal" in the title was frowned upon, and in its placed popped up the Wall Street coffeehouses where stock was bought and sold by members of what would become the New York Stock Exchange. In keeping with an agreement signed out of doors under a buttonwood tree, members of the exchange agreed to deal only among themselves and pay a commission of a quarter of a percent on all trades.

Instead of cutting deals outside on the street, brokers moved inside to the relative comfort of a handful of Wall Street coffeehouses. These coffeehouses simply oozed character, and if Wall Street seems rough and tumble today, one can only say that it came by it honestly. They were classically democratic institutions where the rabble rubbed elbows with the fat cats, and along with trading stocks, people also gathered to gamble, buy and sell slaves, get drunk, pull imaginative swindles, read the papers, sell insurance, brawl, deal in all manner of goods and services, dance, party, talk politics, talk politics loudly, and talk politics even more loudly until the inevitable fistfight broke out. (One thing was said to guarantee a fight at these coffeehouses, and that was the assemblage of more than one person.) Wagons, carts, and people jammed the streets outside, and auctioneers clambered atop barrels of flour or rum and bellowed prices to the crowd below.

In fact, what really got the produce exchanges off the ground was that its traders down at the warehouses wearied of having to walk up to the coffeehouses to tender their orders. The Produce Exchange began life in 1852 as the Corn Exchange, which was built over ground that had been the old market place. Reflecting its deep historical roots, the name evolved from the Dutch Markt-Feldt to Market Field to Marketfield Street, which connected the trading grounds to the wharf where Erie Canal cargo was loaded and unloaded. Two decades later, rapid escalation of trade required a roomier quarters, and when given these marching orders, the architect didn't skimp. George Post responded with an architectural thunderclap, a crimson colossus that looked as if it could balance all that nation's farmland on its impossibly broad shoulders. Economic panics might come and go, but nothing would lay a glove on this economic bulwark.

Not as if anyone could miss it to begin with, on opening day in 1884 the $3 million exchange was all the more conspicuous for the banners and buntings that festooned its walls, and the cascades of plants and flowers showering its halls. The event was marked with excitement to be sure, but there was an eloquent sentiment for the old exchange building that is seldom seen today. There was a wrecking ball in its future to be sure, but the elders of commodities did not, apparently, want the old exchange quarters to think that its service had gone unappreciated.

Exchange President James McGee found a suitable metaphor in oceanic travel: "I think you will understand me feelings when I say that I have thought this morning akin to one who stands upon the deck of a steamer about to make his first voyage across the Atlantic, with bright prospects before him . . . and ready to take your departure, and you have seen the faces that were peering up into your face, and have caught the glance of eyes that were waving the good-byes, and have heard the words of farewell; you have found it difficult to know whether you should continue your journey or not; but the moment must come, the bell must ring, the steamer must start; and here, today, I think I find a scene just like this."

The steamer analogy went on for some time, as McGee picked out faces in the crowd and urged his comrades to build upon the future by remembering lessons learned in the past. Yet the new Produce Exchange was more than symbolic; it truly marked the passing into a modern new era. "Our fathers did not have the telegraph, the telephone or the East River

(Brooklyn) Bridge. Science and political economy are not yet exhausted . . . we shall make the new Exchange grander than the old and shall make it to bring forth things yet invisible." Thus, equally sad and happy, the Glee Club broke into a chorus of "Good Bye, Dear Halls of Old."

Although America was entering the Industrial Revolution, it was, in the waning nineteenth century, still an agricultural nation, and the Produce Exchange, said Carhart, was "the wealthiest and most influential exchange in the country." The new building, he boasted, "has never lost its place as one of the finest buildings in the world dedicated to commerce and trade, and in the eyes of many people its trading floor, as such, has no rival in the world." Deals that a century before had been agreed to outdoors on a city sidewalk were now conducted under a stained-glass skylight that covered a fifth of an acre, in what its founders referred to as a "commercial temple."

There might have been no organization in the country at that point in time with the pride and swagger of the Produce Exchange. Men spoke of its noble character, of its fairness and impartiality. The Produce Exchange had not met a national crisis it could not conquer, be it economic panic or armed conflict. At the height of the Civil War, Gen. Winfield Scott Hancock, recently wounded at the Battle of Gettysburg, drew the largest crowd on the history of the exchange with an appeal for money and manpower. The exchange responded with a network of recruiting stations and funds for hospitals and the families of departing soldiers. Several exchange members themselves fought and died for the cause.

The Produce Exchange gave financial assistance to Chicago as it rebuilt from the great fire of 1871. It helped the nation weather three economic panics, and established relief funds for unemployed cotton workers in England. Produce Exchange members, said its president in 1884 J. H. Herrick, were well aware of capitalists' reputations for hard-heartedness, but in his opinion the men of his organization were the exception: "The close pursuit of money is supposed to blunt the sensibility to human suffering and to develop an intense selfishness; and yet we search our records in vain for one appeal of the sorrowful and suffering unheard, one cry for help unanswered."

The membership could afford to be generous. Each day on the floor, a roar swelled through the hall as men traded wheat, corn, rye oats, barley, flour, cornmeal, hops, hay, straw, seeds, pork, beef, lard, vinegar, turpentine, dried fruits, beans, peas, meat products, tallow, grease, oils, butter, and cheese, in quantities that ran from a cartful to an entire ocean-going vessel. (Samples of all these commodities were abundant in the hall itself, a point that would be central to an upcoming event in 1903.) Everyone had a specialty, be it flour, oil, or coffee. Some men might spend their entire careers dealing in nothing but lard.

One cable from a vendor in Europe to the Produce Exchange was all it took—traders would arrange for the purchase, as well as attending to the details of warehousing, inspections, insurance, freight, and delivery. Today we have the Internet, but in the 1880s there was the Produce Exchange, and there was certainly a similarity between the two. The exchange was where people went to hunt down a particular factoid, no matter how obscure. Whether it be information about a drought in Russia or the latest technology for processing cotton-seed oil, someone in the exchange hall was bound to know the answer. Grocers, bankers, insurance reps, bakers, shippers, brewers, lawyers—all could be found milling about the floor on any given day, looking for information or a tip that might help them get ahead. Further, he advent of steam power and the telegraph shortened distances and made communication immediate. At the time, these advancements were every bit as impactful as the Web.

Along with being commercially significant, the Produce Exchange was politically significant as well. A century after the Revolution, Americans were quicker to criticize the founders than is the case today. Following the Civil War, and what was viewed as the Southern folly of state's rights, the Produce Exchange—which united traders under one roof—represented the victory of centralization and central government. "Out of the civil war the republic came with more power in the general government . . . and on the grave of states' rights has grown up an intense and absorbing sentiment of nationality," observed opening-ceremonies orator Chauncey Depew, somewhat prematurely. It was prior to hedge funds and flash traders that Depew said that centrist capitalism "(P)roves the morality of man, that he always controls the mighty forces which he conjures; he is never their victim, but always their master, and his Frankensteins are the useful servants of his will."

But speaking of Frankenstein, the New York Stock Exchange was growing as well, although perhaps not as spectacularly. By 1817 it had outgrown the Tontine Coffee House and went on to rent space specifically for the trading of securities. It rented various spaces before moving in with the Produce Exchange in anticipation of its own George Post creation on Broad Street.

On a spring day in 1903, it was time for the securities traders to move out of the massive Produce Exchange and into its new quarters.

If the members of the Produce Exchange had shed some wistful tears over their old digs, such was not the case with the stockbrokers, who couldn't get out of the glorified cow palace fast enough. "The leave taking was not tearful, but rather fearful so far as the noise went, and cheerful so far as the market sentiment of the members was concerned," reported the *New York Times* on April 22, 1903. As the close of business neared, the brokers "sang, shouted, whistled, cheered, howled, shrieked and yelled until they were hoarse."

Brokers began to tear down their cubicles and went after the trading posts themselves, which proved to be too securely fastened for destruction by white-collar vandals. Whether the produce brokers meant to join the stock traders in their happiness or whether they were glad to see them go was difficult to say, but eventually the Produce Exchange members joined in the fray. A temporary, eight-foot partition had been built on the floor to separate the two exchanges, and at some point, a produce broker, in true, boys-will-be-boys fashion, reached into one of his sample bags of grain and hurled a fistful over the wall. The broadside was answered with wads of paper, pencils, and anything else that wasn't nailed down. Back came more grains, corn, beans, and oats and then ultimately the nuclear option—flour. The air became thick with foodstuffs and projectiles large and small, accentuated by clouds of white dust. "For some time this comic battle surged back and forth over the partition," the *Times* wrote. "When the gong sounded the closing hour the noise was so great that it could hardly be heard."

The president of the Stock Exchange took the podium to make "some kind of a speech of thank the Produce Exchange," but the cacophony prevented anyone from hearing a word that he said. Eventually the mirth subsided, and the next morning the traders of the Stock Exchange marched as a group from the Produce Exchange to their new home. For its grand opening, the stock exchange resembled an arboretum more than a trading floor, covered as it was with plants, roses, azaleas, hyacinths, and daisies. Flags draped the podium and bands played merrily. It was also, perhaps, a symbolic passing of the torch as the nation's economy moved from agricultural to an industrial base. By the 1950s, membership in the Produce Exchange had dwindled to 20 percent of its turn-of-the-century highs, when it was doing the modern equivalent of nearly a half-billion dollars worth of business a day. By 1957 there was no longer a point to the grand hall, and the produce exchange members, what was left of them, moved out.

Had the Produce Exchange building hung on for another decade it might have been saved on the wings of the preservation movement that followed the demolition of Penn Station in 1963. But shortly after the exchange members moved out it was gone, saved, perhaps, the indignity of being converted into outlet shopping. But like the building itself, an era had become dated. Crowds no longer paid their respects to the service of old buildings, and the ring of the cash register had drowned out grand nineteenth-century orations focusing on character, charity, and fair play. Architectural historian Talbot F. Hamlin, quoted in the *New York Times*, asked angrily whether New Yorkers were "such slaves to economic pressures that they can have no say in what they see, no power to preserve what they love?" Attitudes of course have changed—but not in time to save the mighty Produce Exchange.

CHAPTER 12

New York's New Insane Classes, and the Woman Who Fought for Them

The year was 1888, the place was Pittsburgh, Pa. And the City Board of Lunacy (bureaucracies in those days were less encumbered by political correctness than they are today, and tended to cut right to the chase) had a problem. The problem could be traced directly back to Castle Garden in New York City, a magnificent structure in the Battery where immigrants disembarked prior to the conscription of Ellis Island for that purpose.

Sitting before a congressional panel, Pittsburgh's Robert C. Elliott, director of city charities, testified that his agency had been bombarded with wave after wave of unfortunate people in need of public support including "insane persons, demented people, pregnant women, etc."

The committee chairman winced. "Pregnant women?"

"Yes sir," Elliott answered. "Pregnant women, demented people, decrepit people and an ignorant class of people who should have not been permitted to come into this country."

The average social worker in the late 1800s would have yawned at modern-day complaints of foreign countries packing up their undesirables for export into the United States. Those countries today would be considered amateurs compared to European nations that felt they had quite the satisfactory answer for the handling of their destitute, their rabble, their criminally insane, and anyone generally who was an inconvenience. And it wasn't just foreign governments. Private citizens who were tired of dealing with a floridly psychotic family member would buy a ticket, stick the hapless individual on an ocean liner and basically ship him or her to an unwitting stateside relative.

No one seemed to be embarrassed by this behavior. Irish counties were quite open about the scheme, and went so far as to solicit bids from steamship companies for the transport of paupers and the infirm to America. Such people were supposed to be turned away at Castle Garden, but like the Mexican border today, "supposed to" didn't always work out in any practical sense. Instead, immigration officials found it easier to process one and all, either institutionalize them in New York or farm them out the America's inland cities, including Pittsburgh.

Elliott had an intimate knowledge of this population of new arrivals, since in his official capacity he operated something of an early version of Meals on Wheels, distributing bread, clothing, and a fire-pit's worth of coal to those unfortunates who remained outside because the asylum and almshouses were full.

Among those arriving on American shores was Alfred Naysmith, an insane killer who was put on a boat bound for America by British authorities, who had noticed that the man had a brother in Pittsburgh and felt a strong duty to unify the family. Then there was Mary Shuring, a seventeen-year-old German girl who became pregnant to a man, Barno Gazed, who, like the gentleman he was, saw the wisdom of spending the eleven dollars it cost to put the Atlantic Ocean between his mistress and his wife. Unfortunately for the young lady, the woman in Pennsylvania to whom she was being sent did not appear to want her around any more than Mr. Gazed did, and the poor girl wound up a ward of the state. John Beck was a thirty-year-old man who had lost his mind as a boy and was sent by his sister from County Down in Ireland to a couple of cousins near Pittsburgh. Not thrilled about the new arrival, the cousins threatened to send him back, until the sister sent along enough money to send her brother out to the American West, where he disappeared from the public record. An English woman sent her aging and no longer useful aunt to America; an Irish father sent his addled daughter. Sometimes these unwanted human beings had a relative to receive them, but often they did not.

Castle Garden, now Castle Clinton National Monument in Battery Park, began life as a fort in 1808, built just a stone's throw from the original Dutch fort at Manhattan's tip, which had been built nearly two centuries prior. Castle Garden's military career ended in 1821, and the fort went through a fascinating time as, in no particular order, an opera house, beer garden, theater, park, and exhibition hall. But by 1855, it was apparent that some sort of more orderly processing center for new immigrants was necessary than simply allowing them to disembark on a South Street dock. So Castle Garden was once again enlisted into an official capacity as the Emigrant Landing Depot.

Perhaps eight million immigrants passed through Castle Garden, including Nikola Tesla, Harry Houdini, Sophie Tucker, and Typhoid Mary. Yet even Typhoid Mary would have been Queen Mary compared to some of the miserable creatures who were herded through Castle Garden like animals in a stockyard. The place was in a constant uproar, with great crowds of people shouting to be heard in more languages, dialects, and accents than could be counted. Under the 1882 Immigration Act, passengers were supposed to be examined prior to the entry into the country—convicts, the insane, the destitute, or people who for one reason or another were unable to care for themselves were not, in theory, supposed to be allowed in. But the administration, contended Pittsburgh's Elliott, "was all a farce. There is practically no examination at all. They just drive them through the pen at a trot. I have seen people go through there that I would not admit into this country under any circumstances. If Castle Garden were wiped out of existence, it would be better for Pittsburgh and better for the country at large."

Elliott protested the violation of American immigration laws among Castle Garden authorities in the strongest possible terms, but his complaints fell on deaf ears. At one point, he had his agents return a handful of lunatics to Castle Garden, where the unimpressed bureaucrats simply shrugged and turned them loose into the street.

In the heyday of the corrupt political machine known as Tammany Hall, there were somewhat logical reasons why New

York authorities would find it useful to accept any passenger who was able to stumble off the boat. For a reasonable kick-back, Tammany would steer the immigrant transit business to favored railroads or steamship lines. More importantly, every immigrant represented a potential vote. And considering the political machine's reputation, soundness of mind was not necessarily a quality Tammany would have found to be attractive in a future voter. Tammany ran something of a shadow welfare state that catered to immigrants, buying their loyalty with a job, a loaf of bread, or a few lumps of coal.

As Castle Garden turned a blind eye to illegal immigration, the nation's lunatic asylums as a whole were predictably filled to overflowing, because New York City's own hospitals were unable to handle the load. Equally predictable was that conditions in the city's jam-packed asylums were not the best. New York's first asylum opened on Blackwell's Island (an isle in the East River that in 1971 was later named for Franklin Roosevelt) in 1839. Somewhat ironically, Blackwell's Island Asylum was built as an answer to "miserable" conditions for the city's own mentally ill, who up until that time had been kept in a hospital basement. The result of lax immigration policy was evident in the asylum's population. In 1840, the institution housed fewer than three hundred inmates—in 1870, with no expansion or other improvements, the population stood at thirteen hundred. While immigrants represented less than half of the city's population as a whole, in Blackwell's Island, insane immigrants outnumbered natives by nearly five to one.

As a consequence, there was a limited constituency willing to speak for patients of the institution. To make it even more circular, it was citizens of the nations who had sent the insane to America in the first place who occasionally spoke on their behalf. No less an authority on gloom and despair than Charles Dickens himself wrote in 1842, "I cannot say that I derived much comfort from the inspection of this charity . . . everything had a lounging, listless, madhouse air, which was very painful. The moping idiot, cowering down with long disheveled hair; the gibbering maniac, with his hideous laugh and pointed finger; the vacant eye, the fierce wild face, the gloomy picking of the hands and lips, and munching of the nails: there they were all, without disguise, in naked ugliness and horror." If there were such a thing as a stereotypical madhouse, Blackwell's Island was it.

The inmates, however, were in fact about to get a voice, and once again this voice originated from the area of Pittsburgh.

Elizabeth Jane Cochran was born in 1864 to privilege that didn't last. Her father Michael gave her hometown, Cochran's Mill, its name, and provided the family a good living as a prominent judge. He neglected, however, to write a will, and when he died when she was six, his family could not legally claim his estate. This drove the girl and her mother into the city of Pittsburgh, where they ran a boardinghouse and, meaningfully, kept up with the news by reading the Pittsburgh Dispatch. It was perusing these pages that the eighteen-year-old became incensed at a columnist names Erasmus Wilson. Wilson was one of those men who didn't know as much about women as he thought he did. It was his misfortune to wax unenlightened (in print) about how women wasted their time in school, lest it was to become a useful assistant to her husband as he was about the business of conquering the world—otherwise, it would be better for her to focus her energy on being a good wife, mother, and housekeeper. Cochran had attended a year of school seeking to become a teacher, but the family finances had forced her to drop out. So, naturally, the columnist's comments hit a nerve.

Cochran wrote a scathing rebuttal that caught the eye of the Dispatch editors, who gave her a job (good) and stuck her in the paper's women's section (bad). Still, she was able to do things of note—constricted though she was, she still showed enough initiative to lay the foundation for a career as perhaps the nation's first great investigative reporter. Second, taking a cue from a popular Stephan Foster song, she took on the pen name of Nellie Bly.

Although her historical celebrity comes from a seventy-two-day spin around the globe (bettering Jules Verne's Phileas Fogg), Bly's more important work was in journalism. When Pittsburgh became too small, she set out for New York City, where she found herself in the newspaper offices of the Hungarian born Joseph Pulitzer, who had come to America in 1864 as a recruit to fight in America's Civil War. His paper, the New York World, was a leader in the kind of investigative reporting Bly had come to specialize in, so not long after she went to work for the great publisher, he already had a project in mind that she might be interested in: Would she be willing to fake insanity to get inside the doors of Blackwell's Island, from where she would write an expose on conditions in the city's premier lunatic asylum?

Bly could only think of one question: How did Joseph Pulitzer propose to get her out of the fearsome institution once she had gotten in? Pulitzer acknowledged he hadn't thought that far ahead. It hardly mattered; Bly had the assignment of a lifetime.

Mental institutions in the late 1800s were rife with horror stories, which many people were disinclined—to the extent that they thought about them at all—to believe. After all, public psychiatric hospitals had been born out of the abuses of private, for-profit madhouses, where the more difficult patients would spend their days chained to a basement wall. In England, the Lunacy Act of 1845 established that the mentally ill were to be treated less like inmates and more like patients. That notion was spreading overseas, and by the mid-1800s, a public mental-health institution had opened in Utica, NY, soon to be followed by many others across the country. But the change that came over asylums was spotty and, by today's standards, somewhat counterintuitive. The massive stone, multicupola asylums that have become a staple backdrop for modern horror movies were so built at the time because the architecture was deemed to be soothing to the mentally infirm.

Bly set out to report on conditions inside the walls of Blackwell's Island with the notion that tales of woe were, in her mind at least, greatly exaggerated. Her assignment was to report on conditions exactly as they were—if they were terrible, she'd of course have a better story, but if the asylum were some sort of mental-health success story, that would be interesting to the reading public as well. But first, she had to get inside. "I had little belief in my ability to deceive the insanity experts, and I think my editor had less," she wrote. Bly needn't have worried, because as far as insanity experts were concerned, there appeared to be no such thing.

In the days leading up to her play for incarceration, Bly spent evenings in front of the mirror impersonating the public's image of a mentally ill person. She experimented with bugged eyes, vacuous stares, and any other expression she felt would be of use in a lunatic's facial toolbox. Phase one was to get a room in a boardinghouse for working women, which she achieved easily enough. And from there, one of the lower of New York's social rungs to begin with, the road to the asylum was practically greased. Hard-wired to be wary of any newcomer, the residents soon picked up on Bly's sad countenance and sleepless nights. Her strongest card proved to be a fixation on some fictitious trunks that she claimed had been waylaid in her journey from Cuba—it soon became clear that ranting about lost trunks was her ticket to the island.

But there remained some pitfalls to be dodged. When the boarders could stand her no more, they called for the police, who took her to the station. By bad luck, she had interviewed that particular precinct captain some days prior while working on an unrelated story, and felt fairly certain she would be recognized. But if he did, he made no mention of it. Her next problem was an overly kind judge, who was loathe to institutionalize the attractive young woman. Once again, it was the obsession with the trunks that bailed her out and had her committed to Blackwell's Island.

It became clear that the doctors who examined her were scarcely schooled in the diagnosis of mental illness. They asked a few questions, stared into her pupils, had her stick out her tongue and declared her "totally demented." While this suited Bly's purposes it was a virtual death sentence for other, clearly sane, women who were being processed along with her. As they boarded the boat for the short journey across the river, they were told they were going to "Blackwell's Island, an insane place, where you'll never get out of." And for most of them, insane or not, this intelligence was all too true.

On arriving on the island, Bly and the rest of the women in her group were stripped of their clothes and thrown into a tub of ice cold water, their bodies then scrubbed raw by a grinning inmate. The clothes they were given were far too thin for the late-September cold, and the beds were too hard for decent sleep. Food was limited to cold, discolored tea, malodorous gruel, cold, boiled potatoes, and spoiled beef.

Once a day the women were given comical straw hats and walked like dogs along the institution's sidewalks. On her first such promenade, Bly encountered the hard-core, truly insane inmates who were being similarly exercised. She smelled them before she saw them. "Some were yelling, some were cursing, others were singing or praying or preaching, as the fancy struck them, and they made up the most miserable collection of humanity I had ever seen," Bly wrote in her report. "As the din of their passing faded in the distance there came another sight I can never forget: A long cable rope fastened to wide leather belts, and these belts locked around the waists of fifty-two women. At the end of the rope was a heavy iron cart, and in it two women, one nursing a sore foot, another screaming at some nurse, saying: 'You beat me and I shall not forget it. You want to kill me,' and then she would sob and cry. The women 'on the rope,' as the patients call it, were each busy on their individual freaks. Some were yelling all the while. One who had blue eyes saw me look at her, and she turned as far as she could, talking and smiling, with that terrible, horrifying look of absolute insanity stamped on her. The doctors might safely judge on her case. One woman had on a straightjacket, and two women had to drag her along. Crippled, blind, old, young, homely, and pretty; one senseless mass of humanity. No fate could be worse."

Above it all was an inspirational phrase high on the wall of a pavilion: "While I live, I hope." Yet hope was entirely missing. It was, perhaps one thing for those who were genuinely out of their faculties, but for those who were still reachable, the motto was ferociously absurd. The treatment the women received basically consisted of a doctor going from patient to patient in the sitting room, asking how they felt. Any complaints about food or temperature were met with an understanding nod, at which point the doctor would move on to the next woman, to ask how she was feeling that day. It was the calm and quiet "treatment" of these sitting rooms that were the most cruel. In Bly's words, "What, excepting torture, would produce insanity quicker than this treatment? Here is a class of women sent to be cured. I would like the expert physicians . . . to take a perfectly sane and healthy woman, shut her up and make her sit from 6 a.m. until 8 p.m. on straight-back benches, not allow her to talk or move during these hours, give her no reading and let her know nothing of the world or its doings, give her bad food and harsh treatment, and see how long it will take to make her insane. Two months would make her a mental and physical wreck." That would happen fairly frequently, since a number of patients should never have been there in the first place, but were institutionalized because they didn't speak English, or had a physical malady that was mistaken for mental illness.

Strong minds deteriorated, diseased minds lost all sense of reality. In the night, women prayed for death, screamed that they were being murdered, begged for blankets and cried out for the police. During the day, complaints of inadequate food or clothing were met with the same refrain: They owed their existence to charity, so they should be glad for what they had. Anyone who acted out was beaten with broomsticks or suffocated with blankets. Clean clothes were issued only once a month, unless the inmate was expecting a visitor. Baths came once a week, with all the women of the ward forced to use the same towels and bathwater. The infirm were teased and chided for sport in a manner their reinforced their insanity.

Bly made a point of acting like her sane, normal self during her stay on Blackwell's Island, but only one doctor had an inkling she was not afflicted. "I always made a point of telling the doctors I was sane and asking to be released, but the more I endeavored to assure them of my sanity the more they doubted it," she wrote. Of course the paper's attorneys did secure her release, which left Bly feeling both relieved and guilty: "I had looked forward so eagerly to leaving the horrible place, yet when my release came and I knew that God's sunlight was to be free for me again, there was a certain pain in leaving. For ten days I had been one of them. Foolishly enough, it seemed intensely selfish to leave them to their sufferings. I felt a Quixotic desire to help them by sympathy and presence. But only for a moment. The bars were down and freedom was sweeter to me than ever."

Bly's subsequent report produced a grand jury investigation, in which she was all too happy to participate. Her testimony was well-received, and she agreed to accompany the twenty-three men on a tour of the island so they could see the atrocities for themselves.

The first inkling that something was afoot came on the boat ride. Instead of the rotting, barely seaworthy tub in which she had initially been transferred, the transportation afforded to the jury was a fine, well-scrubbed craft. In the institution itself, the nasty nurses had been replaced by kind, loving souls. So too had the grimy washbasins and hard mattresses been replaced. In the kitchen, two barrels of salt were on display, along with fragrant loaves of freshly baked bread.

What had happened? Had the institution truly changed its ways, or was this a cosmetic facelift for the benefit of the jury? Bly soon had the answer—the women whose stories she had told to the jury, were missing. Administrators said they had been sent off to unknown locales or denied their existence altogether. So the jury would be asked to choose between the word of a young, female newspaper reporter or a team of men in the health-care profession. In the nineteenth century in such a situation, there was little assurance that justice would prevail.

But in the end, there was too much of Bly's story that rang true, or that couldn't be painted over with cosmetic changes. For one, doctors had no way to explain how they could have allowed a perfectly sane woman to dupe them into believing she was ill. Nor could they say why they continued to believe she was insane, even after she had cast off her performing role as a lunatic. The grand jury believed Bly. As a result, numerous reforms came to Blackwell's Island, and the budget was increased by today's equivalent of $21 million.

Still, this was the beginning of the end for the Blackwell's Island Asylum. By the turn of the century, its patients had been transferred to more modern quarters, and the buildings taken on by Metropolitan Hospital. Metropolitan moved out in 1955, and the abandoned buildings deteriorated, save for the central octagon (since incorporated into an apartment complex) where Charles Dickens found the only thing there was to like about the place—a grand, spiral staircase. Today, the Ed Koch Queensboro Bridge, also known as the 59th Street Bridge, passes over Roosevelt Island, the inspiration for Simon and Garfunkel's *The 59th Street Bridge Song,* better known as—belying the horrors that once played out below—*Feelin' Groovy.*

CHAPTER 13

New York Declares War on Pigs

Foreign visitors to America's greatest city in 1842 were certain to be struck by the equality. Not the equality of man in relation to man, but the equality of man in relation to hog. A wealthy, top-hatted gentleman of great import would command the sidewalk as a general thing, sending artisan, journeyman and beggar alike tripping lightly out of his path. But if a hog were to come trotting down the sidewalk, it was the aristocrat who was forced hop aside. There was no reasoning with a pig.

And there were plenty of pigs in New York prior to the Civil War, just as there were plenty of pigs—well, everywhere. It would have been impossible to travel virtually anywhere in the country without encountering pigs, whose contributions to the nation's menus excused their bad behavior on its city streets.

From an intelligence standpoint, there was little difference between a pig and a dog. A pig could be let loose during the day to forage for food (which was plentiful in the mounds of garbage that littered the city) and it would dependably return home to its owner at night. Pigs were a tremendous source of meat production. Not only did they find their own food, but they also reproduced at a rate generally associated with rabbits. Whereas a cow might have one calf a year and that calf would take two years to mature, a pig could have a litter of 10 every four months, with the piglets ready for the table after just six months. To poor families scratching to get by, pigs were a key to survival.

There was also a commercial aspect to the animals, as butchers—particularly in New York's "Hogtown," a neighborhood between 50th and 59th streets from Fifth to Eighth Avenue—kept the swine in porcine flophouses known as "piggeries" at night and turned them loose during they day. It was something of a tradeoff. While the pigs would indeed eat down rotting piles of garbage, entrails and the occasional rotting corpse of a dog or horse, what they left in their wake was no bed of violets.

Just as fearsome as the pigs themselves were their keepers, who tended to be strapping immigrant women who did not make it across the Atlantic by being soft. In the Old World, raising a few pigs was considered grist for the housewife, the guidelines outlined in the likes of an 1844 British publication, Farming for Ladies: A Guide to the Poultry-Yard, the Dairy and Piggery. Women who followed his guidelines, the author assured, "will find it not only adds largely to the comforts of her family, but (will) derive from it also a source of pleasure to herself, of which no 'town-lady' can form an idea."

Not exactly. At least not in New York City, where plenty of town ladies had the pleasure, if that's indeed what they called it. But the point was that anyone was free to take a woman's pigs when they pried them from their cold dead hands. That held as well for the increasing number of outright hog farms that more or less operated in the heart of the city. Along with the hogs, these urban farmers operated rendering plants that melted down all nonedible parts of the hog, along with bones, hides, offal and any other organic delicacy that the city's wretched mass of destitute barrel pickers might provide them with in exchange for a penny or two. These plants were part and parcel to all the charms outlined in Upton Sinclair's book The Jungle, in which Chicago stockyard processors bragged that they used every part of the pig except the squeal.

New Yorkers, in one form or another, had been fighting urban pigs for two full centuries without result, but all that was about to change. The first catalyst—there were two—arrived in the New York harbor on the first day of December, 1848. The liner New York had sailed from France, and on the voyage, seven of the three hundred passengers contracted cholera and died. The remaining passengers were quarantined on Staten Island, and within a month, sixty more were symptomatic and half of those were soon dead. Panic swept through those in quarantine faster than the disease itself, and a number of contaminated individuals escaped into the city.

Cholera had broken out in New York in 1832, feeding on foul water supplies, overcrowded tenements and a general layer of filth that seeped into every aspect of city life, particularly in the poorer, vice-riddled neighborhoods. This came as no particular surprise to city fathers, who associated high mortality with low morality—disease, they believed, spread not because of unsanitary living conditions, but because of unsanitary souls. Except, as the death toll climbed to eighty in June and twenty-five hundred in July—the epidemic would kill more than five thousand that summer—more and more people started to believe that the cause just might be the pigs.

The second strike against swine turned out to be Central Park, the southern end of which was essentially ground zero for the city's piggeries (ironically enough, Hogtown essentially occupied the neighborhood that is currently called home by the Ritz Carlton et al.) While the city leaders were more or less content to turn their back on the problem of pigs and the associated rendering plants when it primarily affected Irish and German immigrants, attitudes changed when more upscale neighborhoods were impacted.

If Central Park were designed to be an everyman's retreat, such would not be the case with the real estate that surrounded it. "As the uptown neighborhoods around the newly designed Central Park rose in value, the piggeries were becoming a liability," wrote Catherine McNeur in the New York Post. "As New Yorkers who lived downtown took carriages and streetcars to visit the new park, they had to cover their noses with handkerchiefs as they passed through Hogtown. Some feared that the odors wafting from the pigsties and cauldrons were making New Yorkers sick."

McNeur, author of Taming Manhattan: Environmental Battles in the Antebellum City, also noted that not only the hogs, but the immigrants, had become an issue—residents of the increasingly upper crust neighborhoods were inclined toward snarky comments that it was growing difficult to tell the people who owned the pigs from the pigs themselves. In the end, more than public health, it was probably this anti-hog gentrification that spelled doom for the piggeries, and prompted what became grandly known as the New York City Piggery War of 1859.

According to the *New York Times*, Hogtown was taken by storm by eighty-seven armed officers on July 26. With pickaxes and crowbars they smashed hog pens, much as their descendants would demolish distilleries more than a half-century later. With military precision, two divisions marched up Sixth and Seventh avenues and finally approached the neighborhood "whose summit is crowned by the castle—if it be true that every man's shanty is his castle—of James McCormick, the king of the offal boilers."

Police didn't expect McCormick to go quietly into the night. His property protected by a phalanx of junkyard dogs and with available manpower from neighboring, sympathetic firefighters, McCormick had promised to shoot any man who touched any one of his two hundred hogs. When the police arrived, however, McCormick meekly agreed to divest himself of the pigs and cooperate with authorities.

From piggery to piggery the city inspector's men went, driving away hogs, breaking up pens and spreading lime to do battle against the stench. Typical was the shanty of Patrick Bohen: "Here, as in other places," the *Times* wrote, "the officers of the law entered, and amid the barking of dogs, the jabbering of Hibernian females, the noise of falling rubbish and the grunting and squeaking of swine, plied their pickaxes and crowbars, scattered the disinfecting agent by the pailful and drove out the pigs. The latter was by far the most difficult operation that they had to perform." Anyone who has ever had the misfortune of trying to catch a pig barehanded would understand the problem. Pigs are quick, stubborn, unspeakably strong, and earsplittingly loud when being coerced to do something against their wishes.

Pigs would refuse to exit their pens, requiring officers to crawl in with them and manhandle the animals into the street, at which point the pigs would often as not escape for the safety of a neighboring pen. All this was enjoyable, if to no one else, to the reporters for the city papers. "It was laughable to see the Superintendent of Sanitary inspection, who did not hesitate to perform his share of the unpleasant manual labor of the expedition, twisting the tail of an overgrown porker around his hand, while one of his assistants seized the animal by the ears, and pulling and tugging and slipping and sliding over the filthy, slimy floor of the pen, until by dint of persevering endeavor an ejectment was effected."

If the majority of the piggery owners were resigned to being put out of business, their frying-pan-wielding wives were less charitable, causing only slightly less commotion than the pigs. "Very poor revinge, to tear down people's buildings after the pigs is all sent away intirely," said one Irish wife. "Very shabby for gentlemen; gentlemen wouldn't do it." Her husband was more philosophical. "Och, let them knock 'em down; we'll sue 'em for it." Another self-described "poor widow" was taking it all in, and might have escaped detection had not an ample hog she had secreted under her bed let loose with an untimely grunt. The pig was rousted out, and another, but as they searched her one-room shanty police were at something of a loss how to deal with the half dozen chickens who shared the woman's bed.

By noon, the officers decided to rest their case on the morning's work, and retired to a nearby saloon from which they gave the remaining piggery owners a day to clean up and clear out, lest they suffer the same fate as those whose establishments had faced the wrecking bar. Most willingly, if grudgingly complied, spelling a quick end to the New York Piggery War of 1859.

CHAPTER 14

A Floating City of Liquor

In the late morning of December 3, 1925, nearly fifty lawmen fanned out across Manhattan, visiting offices on Lexington Avenue, in Grand Central Terminal and at the East River National Bank, taking more than a dozen men into custody. When a Coast Guard cutter docked at the Barge Office on the Battery later that evening, four officers were arrested as they stepped off the boat. It was, the government said, "the greatest roundup in the history of Prohibition."

The feds had busted an international rum ring led by noted gangster William Vincent "Big Bill" Dwyer, who, despite a mountain of evidence against him, did not seem terribly worried about his predicament. At his arraignment he swaggered into the courtroom, grinning ear to ear and flashing several large diamonds and a gem-studded swastika ring. Dwyer was charged with stashing more than four thousand cases of liquor in the coal bunkers of the steamship *Augusta*, and buying off Coast Guard officers who looked the other way when the *Augusta* was chugging up the Hudson River on its way to Yonkers. For these poorly paid government sailors, the temptation had been too much. For two years, they'd been guests at Dwyer's Sea Grill restaurant on West 45th Street, where cash was liberally passed around and the men, prosecutors said, "were feasted and entertained with wine, women and song." Prosecutors were careful to praise the majority of Coast Guard members who remained loyal to their agency, even thought their own pay of thirty-six dollars to one hundred dollars a month was dwarfed by the $1,000 their dishonest brethren were paid just to let a single ship sail unmolested into the harbor.

Dwyer's attorney insisted that the charges were "pure romance," and that his client was a hard working man interested only in putting bread on the table for his family. The G-men rolled their eyes. Just two months prior they'd been chasing Dwyer in his armor-plated speedboat, exchanging gunfire and terrifying commuters being ferried to Manhattan. Even two-bit smugglers were coming to the feds complaining about Dwyer, who was also running a bootleg protection racket on the side, charging smaller smugglers two dollars a case to stay in business. Dwyer had also been heard to gloat that off-loading liquor on a New York pier was as easy as unloading tomatoes.

Prohibition, which began in 1920, defined the years between World War I and the Great Depression. Many an irritated Doughboy blamed women and pacifists for ushering in Prohibition while they were off fighting a war. "By the time we got home it was too late," one remarked. But in many respects, liquor was only a small part of the story—drinking more or less went on uninterrupted, and by most historical accounts the flow of booze actually increased at the time. The twenties weren't called "Roaring" for nothing. But in New York City, the Eighteenth Amendment created an independent biosphere fueled by liquor, where economics, society, crime, and international relations played off each other in their own separate world.

Dwyer's life, for one, was turned upside down by the Volstead Act. Before Prohibition he was a common dockworker from the Irish slum of Hell's Kitchen. On the waterfront, he had access to shipping, trucks, and garages, a perfect bootlegger toolbox. Dwyer parlayed the assets of transportation into an empire, with a fleet of ships that transported millions of dollars worth of hooch from Europe to American shores and distributed it through a network of bootleg jobbers.

Prohibition created a breadth and depth of crime that was certainly not intended by the temperance movement, and turned many a good man to the bad. "This bribery, corruption, perjury and prostitution of government officials is the most serious phase of the failure rigidly to enforce prohibition against the rich men at the top who accumulate fortunes by their organized and highly syndicated violation of the laws," said United States Attorney Emory Buckner.

Antidry leagues popped up with "wet petitions," asking that Prohibition be abandoned, not necessarily because they were thirsty for drink, but because the criminal and moral condition of the city had become much worse under the law. One bootlegger, whose ship had sunk when it hit an iceberg, lamented that he could buy off the authorities, but he couldn't buy off an iceberg.

But perhaps the most bizarre element of Prohibition in New York City, was a line of ships, a floating city that hung just off the coast in international waters called Rum Row, a staging area off of Long Island and northern New Jersey for smugglers who would offload cases of liquor from these foreign-flagged ships and pack them into speedboats for a daring run to some remote shoreline. From there, the liquor would often go to a cutting plantwhere one case of liquor would magically become three.

Most liquor sold in the twenties was produced domestically in stills and bathtubs across the country. And most international smuggling occurred overland from Canada. But nowhere did Prohibition so closely resemble a cross between a game of chess and open warfare as it did on Rum Row.

Rum Row was a sociable place, where people were shot, stabbed, extorted, and conned, where bribes were collected, prices set, and women—who visited Rum Row for the healthful effects that the sea air would have on their skin, ostensibly—were passed around like cigarettes. Rum running was something of a misnomer; most of the liquors were whiskeys, gin (for the women, it was said), or seasonally appropriate champagne and wines. Foreign smugglers guessed the term rumrunner came about because of the newspapers' love for alliteration.

At the time, the hard drinkers of New York City preferred to knock back a shot of whiskey, followed immediately with a swig of water. In such rapid succession was this progression accomplished that amazed foreigners said you could hear the second drink splashing against the first on their way down. The taste of the spirit was not terrible important, since it was downed much at the same speed a dog gulps peanut butter. The effect was what mattered. It was also true in New York City that a drink, while expensive, was not terribly difficult to find. A shot might cost today's equivalent of six dollars, but it was not hard to locate a bartender who would pour you one from a bottle hidden by a row of soft drinks that were mainly for show. The only way the customer could be assured he wasn't getting a drink cut with wood alcohol or formaldehyde was to buy the bartender a drink at the same time—this clever safeguard always assured the barkeep would produce a bottle of the good stuff.

The credit for Rum Row is generally assigned to Capt. William S. McCoy, a teetotaling shipbuilder from Florida whose business was succumbing to the burgeoning motor-freight industry. McCoy is mostly presented as the White Knight of Rum Row, perhaps largely because he took responsibility for his own press clippings, writing extensively about his bootlegging experiences. McCoy was one of the few who was proud of the quality of his drink, and because he refused to cut his liquor with water, his spirits was said to be the source of the phrase "The Real McCoy"—although similar catchphrases appeared in literature more than a half-century prior. His biographer, Frederic F. Van de Water wrote, "The liquor McCoy's ships carried to Rum Row was always the best. Debts he incurred, whether oral or written, were paid on time and in full. Friends whom he made, he kept. Persistently he struck at the law of his country, but he held to his own not inconsiderable moral code."

McCoy was responsible for the basic business model that got around the major obstacle to maritime bootlegging: the slow and obvious process of docking and off-loading a ship filled with booze. US authorities had jurisdiction over American-flagged ships within American waters, a problem McCoy solved in May of 1921, when he flagged his schooner *Tomoka* in Britain and anchored it three miles off the coast of Long Island. Then he hung out the Open for Business sign and waited. At night, tiny boats that could negotiate the shallows would line up to take on as much liquor as they could hold, then dart away into the preferably moonless night for a remote cove.

The idea caught on with amazing quickness, and soon an entire wholesale "liquor fleet" was anchored off the New York shoreline, an event that caught the Coast Guard and the US government flat-footed. Even without the problems of corruption, the Coast Guard was scarcely equipped to deal with these innovating bootleggers. It had a total of four thousand men responsible for what amounted to a handful of slow old tubs that were designed more sentry duty than to go buzzing in hot pursuit of light and fast rumrunners. Indeed, the Coast Guard's mission at that point was mainly to perform safety inspections, rescue people in distress, and patrol the Arctic Ocean.

The Coast Guard was up against a fleet of "mother ships" that Prohibition Commissioner Roy Haynes estimated to number in the hundreds up and down the Atlantic Coast. And that many more hundreds of skiffs were circling the mother ships like moths, waiting their turn to load up.

It didn't help law-enforcement efforts that there was little enthusiasm for Prohibition in the overly thirsty cities of New York and Boston. New York had passed the Prohibition amendment reluctantly, and it had more to do with residual anti-German sentiment remaining from World War I (Germans and breweries being almost synonymous) than with a distaste for liquor. North of Long Island, the state of Connecticut hadn't passed Prohibition at all and its citizens weren't keen on starting up some alcoholic version of Neighborhood Watch. In New London, Connecticut, a disrespectful radio operator set up shop within sight of the Coast Guard base itself warning smugglers of its activities. Even the courts took a boys-will-be-boys attitude toward the smugglers, and the Coast Guard was more inclined to continue on with its life-saving job rather than enforce an unpopular law. Rum-running boats that were seized by the government were auctioned off for peanuts, and often as not purchased by their original owners who immediately put them back into service, scarcely missing a round. One ship was seized, auctioned back to the smugglers, and returned to service four times in one year.

Obviously, these smugglers were not in the habit of keeping records (with the notable exception of that "goody two shoes" outlaw McCoy) so it's hard to say how much hooch flowed through the hands of Rum-Row sailors. But a military history of Prohibition by Donald L. Canney notes that the liquor exported out of the Bahamas in 1917 amounted to fifty thousand quarts. By 1922 that amount had skyrocketed from fifty thousand to ten million. The profit on this product helped justify the risk. A case of Scotch that cost eight dollars wholesale could fetch sixty-five dollars on Rum Row before it was cut and cut again, at which point it would be sent to the consumer. "There is general agreement that the early years of the Coast Guard's interdiction . . . were marked only by scattered successes," Canney wrote. "Some say that no more than five percent of the US bound liquor was stopped" between

1921 and 1925. The rumrunners had good lawyers, and, more often than one might think, sympathetic judges on their side. Incredibly byzantine court battles broke out, not just over what could and couldn't be done in international waters, but in domestic waters as well. A bootlegger was arrested on the Hudson River and tried in New Jersey, because both New York and New Jersey were considered co-owners of the river—except that a sharp attorney, relying on some dusty old lawbook, discovered that while both New York and New Jersey did indeed own the riverbed, the water that was in it was exclusively the property of New York. A friendly judge agreed, giving bootleggers yet another advantage.

In the early days of Rum Row, nor'easters claimed more boats than did the government. In coastal communities during heavy storms, there was no more popular occupation than—sensing the imminent demise of a rumrunner on the shoals—standing on the shoreline in hopes of snagging a few cases of the doomed ship's cargo.

And on the ships themselves, characters abounded. Charles A. Smith, a witness in the William Dwyer trial, recounted how he married a woman he had known for six weeks in November 1924, and spent an hour with her before sailing off to Rum Row. The next time he saw her was in April 1925, as she greeted him with divorce papers. Part of the problem, perhaps, was that three days after the wedding, Smith threw a grand, champagne-soaked wedding reception—but failed to invite his new bride. Asked why he had married her in the first place he shrugged and said "For the same reason any man wants to marry a girl." Smith made $40,000 (about $5.5 million in today's dollars) in two years and paid no tax, he testified later, because he thought that only "voting citizens" were required to pay taxes, and since he didn't vote, he was therefore exempt.

At the opposite end of the social spectrum on the row were English gentry who warmed to the sport of it all. Maj. Eric Sherbrooke Walker, Oxford educated and a World War I prisoner of war, he fought with the White Army against the Bolsheviks and got in the game of American bootlegging partly for the money and partly for the adrenaline rush.

Nothing about the Germans or the Bolsheviks could have prepared him for the terror and violence of Rum Row. Frighteningly profane and beastly men sprayed gunfire in his direction, shadowed him in the dark of night, took his money, and sabotaged his boat. And those were the guys who were on his side. He recounted his experiences in the book *The Confessions of a Rum-Runner* under the pen name of James Barbican, a work the *New York Times* found to be disturbingly authentic: "His journal is a record of corruption and double crossing, lying and violence in every party having anything to do with prohibition."

Walker fell in with a gang of men who, lacking pure water, brushed their teeth with beer. They grew progressively drunker through the day as they ran their motorboat into the side of the mother ship, fought off hijackers, and carelessly flicked the ashes of their cigarettes in the direction of open bottles of gasoline. After the first day of going from crisis to crisis, Walker reflected that "Personally I think whiskey is an unpleasant beverage, but there are occasions where it is comforting and this was one of them."

He grew more cynical of the whole Prohibition experiment as time went by, finally referring to it as a "farce," and noting that whiskey and gin flowed in the homes of eight in ten congressmen, even as the law was creating carnage on the high seas. Walker survived his adventures and moved to Kenya where with his bootlegging profits he opened the Treetops Hotel featuring a wildlife-viewing rooms in the canopy. It was here that Princess Elizabeth was staying in 1952 when she learned of the death of her father. Walker commented that he supposed it to be the first time in history that a woman had climbed a tree as a princess and descended as queen.

In the bars, liquor and stories flowed with equal strength. Guffaws were shared over crews that, predictably perhaps, became so hammered on their own cargo that they failed to even notice when the Coast Guard was boarding them. Canney recounted the story of the Norwegian steamer *Sagatind*, which "was boarded and found with 43,000 cases on board, along with $26,000 in cash, and cases piled on deck. No resistance had been met by the Coast Guard boarders: the crew had been 'sampling' the merchandise and was collectively stupefied." In her book *Smugglers, Bootleggers, and Scofflaws; Prohibition and New York City*, Ellen NicKenzie Lawson tells a delightful story of a New Year's Eve off the New Jersey Coast, when Guardsmen boarded a coal barge because they herd the crew "singing lustily," so loud in fact that they were heard by a passing patrol boat. The crew had gotten into the cargo, which included not just coal but cases of champagne.

By the middle of the decade, however, things began to change. If there had ever been a quaint, homespun angle to the bootlegging business, it was gone now. Too much money was at stake. By 1925, one motorboat load of whiskey was worth a staggering $400,000 in today's dollars. More and more frequently, smugglers were turning up dead, and occasionally Coast Guard officers were as well. Bootleggers' wives, who had been able to sleep peacefully at night, now stayed awake, as the odds of their husbands' safe return from a nightly run grew longer. The average bootlegging Joes were getting squeezed on both sides, by the government and by a new, uglier breed of criminal. William McCoy, after serving a nine-month boot-legging prison term, up and quit. It wasn't that prison had reformed him, de Water wrote, but that "the trade has changed and that it no longer is fun. Also, by his own unique yet rigid ethics, it has become too dirty, too wholly crooked. . . . What was once a marine combination of tag and blind-man's buff, with the revenue cutters forever 'it' and each individual run-ner working for himself; what was once a sport as well as a lucrative enterprise has become Big Business with the small independent tradesman absorbed or frozen out." This was quite a populist viewpoint from a convicted kingpin, but there seemed to be some sincerity to it. Bands of hijackers formed to steal from the outlaws who were running liquor. Occasionally these "honest" rumrunners became so incensed with being robbed at the hands of pirates that they sailed into the New York harbor and turned states evidence. Leave it to capitalist America to spoil a wholesome, homespun cottage industry as bootlegging.

On the seas, bootleggers and Coast Guard officers strug-gled to stay one step ahead of their adversaries with increasing intensity. In the courts, laws governing international trade were twisted in new and interesting ways. Unable to block-ade the shoreline, someone got the idea that the Coast Guard might successfully blockade the mother ships themselves.

Boats that were stocking the ships on Rum Row with food and water were seized by the government on the grounds that they did not have the proper licenses to engage in international trade—the mother ships being awarded, for legal purposes, the status of a foreign port. International law that had protected the ships on Rum Row from seizure was now preventing their crews from eating.

If the Coast Guard was slow to rise to the bootleggers' challenge, by the mid-twenties it had begun to catch up. Congress appropriated money for hundreds of boats and more than doubled its manpower. If hundreds of boats were present in Rum Row, the Coast Guard would dispatch equal hundreds of patrol boats. The *New York Times* compared this to man-to-man defense in a sporting event. If there were no law against a foreign schooner anchoring off our shores, similarly, there was "nothing to prevent a United States Coast Guard vessel from spending the day in cruising nonchalantly around said schooner." Where the Coast Guard had previously been forced to devote its resources into chasing down the bootleggers' speedboats, it now concentrated on the "line of scrimmage," to thwart the boats that were ferrying the liquor to shore.

It was a necessary change in tactics, since picking off the small motorboats one by one was virtually impossible. First, there were too many of them. While the Coast Guard might keep track of hundreds of Mother Ships, it could never match the thousands that were at the disposal of the bootleggers. Second, the bootleggers' boats were just too fast. A generation of gearheads who had grown up with the internal combustion engine were having a blast shoehorning big, 300-horsepower airplane engines into the bellies of light, stripped-down hulls.

The US government also renegotiated its seaside boundaries, declaring that domestic waters extended for twelve miles instead of three. This did effectively push back the line of mother ships, but not always with the intended results. The smaller Coast Guard cutters didn't have the range or durability to harass the rum boats so far out to sea. Even new ships soon needed repairs, and the rumrunners' effective network of spies and coded messages knew every time a government boat was relegated to dry dock. The added buffer also spread the field, giving rummies more room to maneuver. A favorite tactic was to radio in a fake distress call that gave the rumrunners a chance to operate when the Coast Guard cutter steamed off to answer the nonexistent emergency.

Every new government tactic or ship was quickly answered by the bootleggers, who often had the sympathy of the public on their side. The *New York Daily News* reported that a popular sport among Coney Island sprectators was to "cheer as motorboats came roaring past them with the revenue cutters in hot pursuit." When the Coast Guard appropriated big, fast Navy destroyers that could run down the smaller motorboats, smugglers used smoke bombs to disguise their maneuvers, then reversed course. The destroyers were fast, their size took forever to turn around, giving the runners a chance to make a getaway. To hide their cargo, smugglers would cover cases of whiskey with mountains of fish. When the government got wise, they built false bottoms in the hulls of their boats. Soon the Coast Guard had charts of all popular boat models and could sniff out holds with suspicious dimensions, so the smugglers built cargo boxes underneath the hull. Others filled torpedoes with liquor and propelled them to shore.

The government finally had enough of the fun and games. The Treasury Department issued a statement that "The Administration is determined to make every effort with the material it has to combat and, if possible, to break up the rum fleets which have become a national disgrace off our coasts." But for every battle the Coast Guard won, it became clearer that winning the war was not possible. After a concerted effort with its new fleet of ships, authorities reported that Rum Row ships along the New York City shore had been depleted from seventy to fewer than a dozen. However, although the government might scatter the ships on Rum Row and even restrict the flow of liquor into the city, the price went up and ever more smugglers rushed in to take advantage of the fatter profits.

By 1926, the Treasury Department declared that Rum Rows had been "wiped out," which turned out to be another premature declaration along the lines of Mission Accomplished. Even as Prohibition was set to end in 1933, rum boats salivated like hungry dogs off the New York coast. Three weeks before Christmas, wrote the *New York Times*, "With stores, hotels and restaurants throughout the city hurrying preparations for repeal, hundreds of thousands of gallons of legal liquor and wine are being rushed here on ships and special trains." A twenty-four-car freight train carrying one hundred seventy-five thousand gallons of wine rattled east from California, while legally sanctioned ships aimed for New York harbors with holds filled with Scotch, ports, sherries, Irish whiskies, wines, cognac, vermouth, champagnes, and cordials. "Every agency than can bring wines and liquor to this city legally is being utilized. On or after Tuesday afternoon, there will be a steady flow of liquor in New York City," the *Times* assured its readers.

New York Police Commissioner James Bolan, perhaps engaging in a bit of wishful thinking, said he was not expecting any trouble, "because most of those inclined to celebrate are not in a financial position to do so." Left unsaid was the understanding that the wealthy had never really been deprived in the first place. Nevertheless, Bolan called for a strong police presence in Times Square and on Broadway to discourage any "undue enthusiasm." Thousands of businesses applied for licenses to sell liquor, and speculators bought empty storefronts in anticipation of entering the business of selling alcoholic beverages. Licenses were awarded to hotels and restaurants, as well as to Bloomingdale's and Gimbel's department stores. Macy's announced that it would have forty experts on hand to help the clientele make intelligent selections; these experts included a Dutch baron, a French count and a former officer of the Czar's Imperial Military College.

While the repeal of Prohibition did incite the predictable partying, the more pronounced effect was political. The day that brought repeal had much the same flavor that an epic Supreme Court decision on a major social issue would today. The Women's Organization for National Prohibition Reform called it "a great victory for constitutional government." Repeal was seen as a plank in the New Deal that promised better days ahead in all manner of social and economic arenas. The temperance movement, meanwhile, lashed out with renewed fury. "In thousands of places today," thundered Fred Victor, New York superintendent of the Anti-Saloon League, "individuals will be advertising themselves as inadequate, if not plain yellow. The moral coward drinks in order that he may escape the stern realities of modern existence (or) because he has not sufficient moral and spiritual resources to make him adequate for the demands of this tremendous day."

Liquor, of course, was not the final nail in America's coffin any more than it was an economic development incentive. The truth was somewhere in the middle. In the hinterlands, there was anecdotal evidence that Prohibition was a service to families and was a boon to productivity (or at least dependability) in the workforce. But in New York City it had failed miserably. Crime, and even drinking itself, escalated. Prohibition was blamed for increasing drunkenness among women and teenagers, who succumbed to the appeal of the forbidden fruit. Prohibition created crime where there had been no crime before, and millions of tax dollars were spent fighting it. Even the once cocky Rum Row kingpin Big Bill Dwyer was humbled. He lost his health in prison, and while he found a second career owning and promoting professional sports teams (including the Brooklyn Dodgers of the National Football League), he was never the same. "I wish I had never seen a case of whisky," he lamented. "I spent years in daily fear of my life, always expecting to be arrested, always dealing with crooks and double-crossers, and now look at me. My wife is heartbroken and I am worse than broke."

CHAPTER 15

A Lake Gets Its Revenge on Manhattan

In the center of Lower Manhattan, surrounded by blocky judicial buildings, is Collect Pond Park, a modest scrub of greenery that, until its recent renovation, was widely disparaged as a decaying urban wasteland useful only to people down on their luck who were disinclined to seek out more formal restroom accommodations. As picturesquely described by Tribeca Trust, "The old Collect Pond Park most New Yorkers remember from serving jury duty nearby was a windswept, raised plaza in the 'Brutalist' style. It was a place loved only by rats and pigeons. It was a park so unloved it spawned a recent redesign to replace the blank expanses, heaving pavers and sinkholes."

The renovation has drawn mixed reviews—an improvement, certainly, with some noteworthy design features, but still not a place frequented by those who do not take their lunch from a bottle. Seeking something nice to say about the square block of open space, the Trust opined that it "look(s) good from a helicopter," but otherwise felt it added little to the streetscape. The homeless and the pigeons began to drift back in.

But had everything gone perfectly with the (ongoing) renovations, it hardly would have befitted the three centuries of history in that particular space, which at times had been of the most beautiful, most industrious, most hideous, and most decrepit part of the town—not to mention the site of what was arguably America's first stab at economic stimulus efforts and New York City's first traffic jam.

Today it is known as the Civic Center in Lower Manhattan, a collection of court buildings between Chinatown and the Financial District. The criminal-justice pedigree extends back two centuries or more, to the days when public stocks and pillories are scrupulously varnished and oiled, and the office of Public Whipper was a singularly prestigious and sought-after post—until the men who held it became so drunk and corrupt through the years that the whipper was often more debauched than the whippee.

But in the beginning, the area was the site of a pond, a small lake really, of fifty acres, with another seventy acres of salt marshes at its outlets. From the start, Collect Pond might have suffered from its hardened, unattractive name, "Collect" being a bastardization of a consonant-heavy Dutch word referring to a reef of shells discarded by Native Americans over the centuries that formed a chalky point jutting into the water. "Kalchhook" was whittled down to Kalch, then Callech, then

Colleck and finally Collect. The Indians, usually so good in these naming matters, failed to leave anything that stuck, even though the lake was a popular resort in their time, and home to a collection of wigwams. In the latter half of the 1600s after the arrival of the Dutch, it was a postcard in waiting, a lake nestled in low, rolling hills, whose shoreline was dressed in a scattering of trees, church steeples, and a handful of trim, two-story cottages, their surrounding meadows neatly divided by attractive wooden fencing. A brook babbled leisurely out of the lake's north end, crossed by a charming stone bridge.

The Collect served for many years as the source of New York's drinking water. Just prior to the Revolution, the city built a holding tank east of Broadway between White and Pearl streets that was thirty feet in diameter that could hold "20,000 hogsheads" of water. It was fed by wooden pipes that ran from the pond to the tank, and from there wagons could fill up to carry water to the drier parts of town. It was such a thriving business that water peddlers and their wagons jammed the area around the reservoir's pump causing citizens to complain and forcing the city to raise and extend the spout so that other traffic could get by as the water wagons filled up.

The pond was a delightful source of recreation in both summer and winter, a popular boating, skating, and picnicking destination and the source of the city's supply of ice. In 1874, Charles Sutton wrote, "It scarcely seems credible to the present generation, unfamiliar with the original topography of Beautiful Manhattan, that there was once a lovely and picturesque lake . . . surrounded by romantic hills, which, in the west, in the vicinity of Broadway, rose to considerable height . . . This fresh water pond remained one of the peculiar features of the natural scenery of the island for upwards of one hundred years after the first settlement. During that period it was the favorite resort of fishermen and sportsmen."

This didn't last, obviously.

The city was growing, south to north, and by the mid-1700s, streets and businesses were eating away at the quaint flavor of the neighborhood. The population to the south made a point of driving out the noxious tanneries, which took up residence on the lake's shores, along with breweries, slaughterhouses and other industries that consumed large quantities of water and were also thrilled with the prospect of dumping bones, offal, and fermented grain into the drink, where they would be out of mind if not exactly out of sight. The populace did its part too, and the fresh water pond became a repository for coal ash, the contents of chamber pots, broken jars, or even dead animals.

Collect Pond was about to meet its end, even though in the final analysis the little lake wound up having the last laugh. It would, however, have one last day in the sun. Twenty years before Robert Fulton claimed to have invented the steamboat, two quirky American mechanics were racing to become the first to design a vessel that would propel itself upstream sans human assistance. Both John Fitch, of Warminister, Pennsylvania, and James Rumsey, of what is now Berkeley Springs, West Virginia, successfully sailed steamboats in 1787. Fitch's first design employed a dozen unmanned oars driven by cranks, wheels, and arms, and looked more like something out of the mind of Dr. Seuss than Thomas Edison. Rumsey's boat was more elegant, using water jet propulsion. But in the end, alas, it was Fulton who won history's acclaim—even though the Navy League of the United States concluded that "Probably no person has received so much praise, and deserved so little, as Robert Fulton."

The role of Collect Pond in this story came into play in 1794, after Fitch had unsuccessfully toured England and France, trying to drum up support for his new contraption. (In perhaps the world's greatest case of bad timing, Fitch was trying to sell steamboats at the height of the Reign of Terror during the French Revolution to people who were understandably more preoccupied with keeping their heads attached to their persons than they were with a mechanized rowboat.) Back in the States, he unveiled a new design on Collect Pond, a boat driven not by gawky oars, but by a more sophisticated propeller. It was the first time on record that steam power had been mated to a screw propeller. (Fitch had also experimented with paddle wheels, but indicated that they "splashed too much," a flaw that future generations would fix simply by covering the wheel.) On the Collect, in the company of dignitaries who would affirm the events of that day, Fitch introduced water to the twelve-gallon iron boiler, waited for steam to rise and then tooled around the lake three times at a speed of six miles an hour before more water had to be added to the system. It was an impressive demonstration, but one which, sadly for Fitch, generated little excitement outside of the immediate neighborhood. But city residents were impressed, even if no one else was, and the papers debated which was the bigger story: Fitch's steamboat, or the time in 1781 when the future King William IV of Great Britain—visiting New York as a midshipman—had fallen through the ice on the Collect while skating, and nearly drowned.

By the end of the century, it was clear there would be no more boat trials or skating parties on the Collect, which was becoming one big open sewer. It would never again be the subject for the young nation's artists who were once fascinated by its pastoral setting. Complaints began to pour in about the foul stench and gruesome contents of the pond. Something had to be done, but olden politicians were little different from modern ones when it came to improving infrastructure. In 1802, a New York street commissioner by the name of Jacob Brown recommended that the city drain Collect Pond into a canal that would run between the Hudson and East rivers. This, he said, would open up four hundred acres of prime land for development, including the lake itself and adjoining marshlands. But City Hall wasn't interested, and the Collect lived on for another half dozen years.

If assigning blame to one person for the demise of the Manhattan lake, Napoleon Bonaparte would serve as well as anyone. The Napoleonic wars that pitted France against Britain et al., had a profound effect on commercial shipping, not just for the belligerents, but for anyone seeking to do business with one or more of the warring parties—of which, the United States was one. The British in particular treated the Americans rudely, capturing its merchant ships and impressing their sailors into service in the British Royal Navy. Naturally, this high-seas equivalent of punching a kid and taking his lunch money did not sit well among Americans, who demanded some sort of action. Wishing to remain neutral, President Thomas Jefferson decided to engage in commercial rather than military warfare. On December 22, 1807, he signed the Embargo Act into law, a measure that prohibited American ships from trading with foreign nations. The thought was that this would deprive Britain of needed goods, forcing the naval bullies to treat the young nation with more respect.

In the storied career of Thomas Jefferson, this was not among his finer ideas. It made America seem weak and inept, destroyed port city economies and was patently ineffective in achieving its stated goal, as British traders were quick to find successful workarounds. In advocating for a heavy federal hand, Jefferson was of course leaving his limited-government comfort zone, and he sought the Embargo Act's repeal before he left office.

Meantime, in a trade-heavy city such as New York, the results were devastating. With the docks shut down, a significant percentage of the laboring class was thrown out of work and, as a particularly hard winter set in, many were on the brink of starvation. In January 1808, sailors and dock hands marched on City Hall, demanding either bread, or better, a job that would allow them to make money to buy bread for themselves. The city needed to put these men to work, and to put them to work it needed a serious public works program.

All eyes turned to Collect Pond. Here was a government stimulus program waiting to happen. To the west of the lake was a high ridge rising a hundred feet above the lakeshore. Without entirely thinking out the long-term consequences— and over the protests of Pierre Charles L'Enfant (the designer of Washington, DC, began his American career as a New York civil engineer), who thought the lake should be cleaned up and turned into the centerpiece of an epic park, and others who wanted to expand it into an inland port—the city decided to pay its unemployed men five cents a barrow load to literally dig up the mountain and dump it into the unwanted lake. A decade before construction started on the Erie Canal, it was a project the scale of which had never been attempted in the state. On paper it all sounded so good. Men would be put to work filling the pond with, as the city put it, "good and wholesome earth," the economy would get a needed boost, and a public nuisance would be eliminated in the process. It was, the papers said, New York's "first superlative undertaking." In an economic sense the project was a success, but in a practical sense the outcome could have been predicted by any four-year-old boy who has endeavored to stir water into good and wholesome earth. The city had effectively created a fifty-acre mud bog.

An anticipated outcome of the massive project was a flurry of development on the newly reclaimed ground. This eventually happened, but not in a way that had been hoped. The area did for a time attract a respectable class of people and commerce—until it all began to sink. The spongy soil became an odiferous mosquito hatchery that ultimately bred more disease than economic growth. Predictably, those who could afford to do so moved out of the neighborhood, and in short order it had morphed into the infamous, crime- and gang-riddled slum known as Five Points. From the 1820s through 1840s, many victims of the Irish potato famine wound up in Five Points, as did former slaves emancipated when New York abolished slavery in 1827. A number of New York's cholera epidemics were traceable to Five Points, along with other maladies that thrived in crowded, unsanitary conditions. No less an expert on squalor than Charles Dickens, in his celebrated tour of the city in 1842, seemed taken aback by Five Points. Wooden tenements haphazardly nailed together were accessed by rickety outdoor staircases. Inside, floors sagged, beams rotted in the damp conditions left by the old pond and more windows were broken than whole. Dim, drunken eyes greeted Dickens in these "leprous" buildings "reeking everywhere with dirt and filth." Then, in one of the greatest zingers in the history of urban ratholes, Dickens asked if the pigs that roamed the streets "ever wonder why their masters walk upright instead of going on all fours and why they talk instead of grunting."

By the 1830s the new only development that found the Collect grounds fit for use was a new city prison cheerfully known as The Tombs. It was designed by Colonel John Stevens, a Hoboken engineer who had recently completed a tour of Egypt, and incorporated a number of features into the prison to resemble the sepulchers of the ancient pharos—hence the name. Whatever other image The Tombs might have conjured up, it gave the sense of unfathomable heaviness. It appeared almost as one solid square of rock a city block in size, with a few columns, windows and sundry ornamentation scratched into the surface. It was among the first in a sprawling assortment of criminal justice buildings, including the human zoo known as Bummers' Hall, where magistrates attempted to sort out the daily flood of boozy and/or addled vagabonds, gamblers, vagrants, gypsies, tramps, thieves, etc., and apportion them out to, depending on circumstances, the penitentiary, the workhouse or almshouse.

Designers of The Tombs had to have had an inkling that building a zillion-ton edifice on wet, mushy soil wasn't the best of ideas, but for whatever reason they were not deterred. Lacking bedrock onto which to lay a foundation, enormous hemlock trunks were lashed together and sunk into the ground in the hope that they could support the monolithic jail. They couldn't. Shortly after it was built, the walls began to sink in places and they never really stopped. Alarmingly, a four-inch crack appeared from the top of one outer wall to the bottom. At one point, settlement caused a lintel and a portion of The Tombs' ceiling to shear loose from its moorings, narrowly missing the district attorney and his staff. The miracle was that The Tombs lasted better than a half-century before it had to be replaced.

But Collect Pond was not done with the neighborhood. With most every building that went up, it reminded contractors of its previous existence. A century after its demise, the *New York Times* noted that it was still coming back to haunt urban engineers: "They have discovered that the old Collect Pond was merely submerged. For when borings are made to determine whether there are substrata sufficient to support the massive buildings projected for the site, the drills encounter the springs of the old Collect and the water comes gushing up as if the fountains of the deep had been loosed."

In the 1920s, a $6 million, seven-story State Office Building was planned for the site bordered by Centre, Worth, Baxter, and Leonard streets. Borings in search of bedrock found muck, ooze, and sand instead. The drill also brought up a shard of a Dutch teacup sixty feet down, as well as evidence of the old artesian well that long ago had supplied the city with water. But one hundred twenty feet down, there was still no solid rock. The foundation subcontractor revised his cost estimate from $225,000 to $1 million and the State Engineers Office ordered the work to be halted. "A way out of the difficulties is still being sought," the papers said.

The land had originally been proposed for a county court-house, but, sensing trouble, the city sold it to the state for one dollar—and appeared to think it had gotten the better part of the deal. To accommodate its courthouse, the city bought land just to the east, ostensibly out of the clutches of the old lake. But even here, the Collect got its revenge. In excavating the site, engineers backfilled with gravel, a course gravel that was immediately flooded by the pond, which was still undulating below the surface. To combat this, the city was forced to build a double bottom, the lower level effectively being a massive, concrete and steel tub, known in engineering circles as a "boat," two feet thick. "The New York County Court House is an ark of justice," quipped the *Times.*

Of course, if buildings above ground were trouble, the subway was a circus all of its own. The subway tunnel was thirty-five feet below sea level, which was right in the wheel-house of the old Collect. When building the Canal Street Station, contracting crews pumped an astounding ten million gallons of water a day from the excavation—because it was fresh water, the source was easily traceable to the Collect. They could have pumped more, but didn't, on the fear that the whole neighborhood would sink into the ground if the entirety of its watery rug were pulled out from under it. Worse, if they pumped out the full breadth of the lake, a process that would have taken two full years, it was feared that saltwater would invade not just the site of the old lake, but across the width of Manhattan Island through the porous layers of crushed stone that supported the city's growing skyline. Instead, the Canal Street Station was walled off with thick walls of steel and concrete; it opened early in the twentieth century—and promptly flooded. Massive amounts of grout were pumped in to seal the leaks and establish at least an uneasy truce with the Collect. Two decades after it opened the *Times* wrote, "Water still surrounds the Canal Street station, with a pressure so great that if a hole were driven through one of the side walls, a stream would shoot clear across to the other side of the station."

Even if the Collect Pond has now been largely tamed, no one can say it didn't go down without a fight. The recent renovations to Collect Pond Park pay tribute to the old lake, with a shallow reflecting pond to remind one and all of what was once there. The park was dedicated in the fall of 2014, but shortly thereafter the reflecting pool spring a leak and had to be drained. The curse of the buried lake was apparently alive and well.

Sources

The backbone of this work was sketched out from accounts in city newspaper articles, government documents, and period texts. It should be noted, however, that newspapers of a century ago and beyond, were quite different that those we are familiar with today. They had their friends, favored causes, and agendas, and consequently cannot always be depended upon. Period texts suffer some of the same problems, and were often written in defense of, or in support of, a particular person or point of view. As such, modern histories, websites, and historical blogs have contributed to the task of fleshing out these stories.

Following is a bibliography of sources that are of particular interest for those who might wish to read further on each particular topic.

Chapter 1
Haw, Richard. *The Brooklyn Bridge: A Cultural History*. Rutgers University Press, 2005.

Hogg, John Edwin. "'Steve Brodie Airplane Landings," *Popular Mechanics*, 32 (1919): 262–64.

McCullough, David. *The Great Bridge: The Epic Story of the Building of the Brooklyn Bridge*, Simon & Schuster, 2007.

City newspapers include extensive coverage of the Brooklyn Bridge jumpers, and are searchable, generally with subscription. Some of their accounts, however, have been called into question.

Chapter 2
Although Peter Zenger is generally granted hero status in historic texts, he was largely a pawn of colonists with a bone to pick against their governors. These colonists are generally treated kindly in history as well, their side having won.

Crown v. John Peter Zenger. *Historical Society of the New York Courts*, online, nycourts.gov accessed 2015. Includes PDF of *Tryal of John Peter Zenger & c.*—a full court transcript of the proceedings.

Rutherford, Livingston. *John Peter Zenger, His Press, His Trial and a Bibliography of Zenger Imprints.* Dodd, Mead & Co., 1904.

Chapter 3
McCabe, James Dabney. *Lights and Shadows of New York Life.* Text reprints some abortionist advertisements from city newspapers, offering, for example, a "Sure Cure for Ladies in Trouble."

New York Times and other metropolitan newspapers provide extensive coverage of "The Great Trunk Mystery."

Shrady, George F., ed. *The Medical Record; A Semi-Monthly Journal of Medicine and Surgery.* Vol. 6. New York: William Woodward & Co., 1871.

Sutton, Charles. *The New York Tombs, Its Secrets and Its Mysteries*. San Francisco: A. Roman & Co., 1874.

Chapter 4
Bankhead, John Hollis. *Pneumatic Tube Mail Service*; Report of the Joint Commission appointed to investigate the value of pneumatic tube mail service. Washington Government Printing Office, 1919. This is a highly detailed investigation of mail tubes, which reached the (erroneous) conclusion that tube and the automobile mail delivery could co-exist.

Depew, Chauncey. *Leaves from My Autobiography: The United States Senate—Ambassadors and Ministers*. Excerpted by Scribner's magazine, Vol. LXXI, January–June, 1921. Depew's wrote extensively, and his highly entertaining writings can be found in a number of sites. They are most always worth the read, no matter what the topic might be.

Solis, Julia. *New York Underground: The Anatomy of a City*, New York: Routledge, 2005.

Chapter 5
Bell, Whitfield J. Jr. *Patriot-Improvers: Biographical Sketches of Members of the American Philosophical Society* Vol. I., Philadelphia: American Philosophical Society, 1997.

Horsmanden, Daniel. A Journal of the Proceedings in the Detection of the Conspiracy Formed by Some White People in Conjunction with Negro and Other Slaves for Burning the City of New York and Murdering Its Inhabitants. Online, http://law2.umkc.edu/faculty/projects/ftrials/negroplot/journalplot.html accessed 2015.

Chapter 6

Blaisdell, Bob, (ed.). *Great Speeches by Mark Twain*. Mineola, NY: Dover Publications, 2013.

Mark Twain's every move was reported by the New York press, and Twain himself, of course wrote extensively on New York, including in his autobiography.

Chapter 7

Nadel, Stanley. *Little Germany; Ethnicity, Religion and Class in New York City, 1845–80*. University of Illinois Press, 1990.

O'Donnell, Edward T. *Ship Ablaze: The Tragedy of the Steamboat General Slocum*. Broadway Books, 2003.

Chapter 8

Ashmead, H. G. *The Man in the Leather Stockings*. Proceedings of the Delaware County Historical Society, Vol. I, 1902.

New York, City of. *A Complete Guide With Descriptive Sketches of Objects and Places of Interest. Street Directory*. New York: Taintor Brothers, 1890.

Chapter 9

Account of the Terrific and Fatal Riot at the New York Astor Place Opera House. District Court of the United States, Southern District of New York. H. M. Ranney, New York, NY, 1849. Includes list of those killed and wounded.

Hornblow, Arthur. *A History of the Theatre in America* Philadelphia: J. B. Lippincott Company, 1 (1919): 21–40.

Chapter 10

Sutton, Charles. *The New York Tombs, Its Secrets and Its Mysteries*. San Francisco: A. Roman & Co., 1874.

Navy League of the United States. *John Fitch, the first in world's history to invent and apply steam propulsion of vessels through water*. Hartford: R. S. Peck Press, 1012.

Collect Pond Park. New York City Department of Parks and Recreation. nycgovparks.org/parks/collect-pond-park/history

Chapter 11

Bundles, A'Lelia. *On Her Own Ground: The Life and Times of Madam C. J. Walker*. New York: Scribner, 2001.

Rickard, Maxine Elliott Hodges Rickard. *Everything Happened to Him: The Story of Tex Rickard*. Frederick A. Stokes Company, 1936.

Williams, Chad L. *Torchbearers of Democracy: African American Soldiers in the World War I Era*, ebook, University of North Carolina Press, 2010.

Woodlawn Cemetery has an excellent online resource for perusing its residents and their history, www.thewoodlawncemetery.org

Chapter 12

Carhart, E. R. *The New York Produce Exchange*. The Annals of the American Academy of Political and Social Science, Vol. 38, no. 2, American Produce Exchange Markets. Sage, 38 (1911); 206–21.

New York Produce Exchange. Ceremonies on Leaving the Old and Opening the New Produce Exchange. New York Produce

Exchange Building Committee, Franklin Edson, Chairman. May 5th and 6th 1884.

Silver, Nathan. *Lost New York*. New York: Houghton Mifflin Co., 1967.

Whitford, Noble E. *History of the Canal System of the State of New York*. Supplement to the annual report of the State Engineer and Surveyor of the State of New York, fiscal year ending September 30, 1905.

Young, John Russell, ed. *Memorial History of the City of Philadelphia*, Vol. II. New York: New York History Company, 1898.

Chapter 13
Bly, Nellie. *Ten Days in a Mad-House*. Ian L. Munro, Publisher, New York, NY.

United States Congress. Testimony taken in July 1888 by the Select Committee to inquire into the alleged violation of the laws prohibiting the importation of contract laborers, paupers, convicts, and other classes.

Chapter 14
McNeur, Catherine. *Taming Manhattan: Environmental Battles in the Antebellum City*. Cambridge: Harvard University Press, 2014.

Chapter 15
Lawson, Ellen NicKenzie. *Smugglers, Bootleggers, and Scofflaws*. Excelsior Editions. Albany: State University of New York Press, 2013.

Solomon, Professor. *Coney Island Past and Present.* Not about Prohibition, per se, but an amusing history of Coney Island drinking habits. Top Hat Press, 1999.

Van de Water, Frederic. *The Real McCoy.* Reprinted 2007, Flat Hammock Press, Mystic, CT.

Walker, Eric Sherbrooke. *The Confessions of a Rum-Runner.* Written under the pen name of James Barbican. Reprinted 2007, Flat Hammock Press, Mystic, CT.